Living by Faith

The Book of Romans

Volume 3

The
the

Romans 8:1–38

DR. DAVID JEREMIAH

with Dr. David Jeremiah

CONTENTS

About
Dr. David Jeremiah
and Turning Point

D r. David Jeremiah is the founder of Turning Point, a ministry committed to providing Christians with sound Bible teaching relevant to today's changing times through radio and television broadcasts, audio series, and books. Dr. Jeremiah's common-sense teaching on topics such as family, prayer, worship, angels, and biblical prophecy forms the foundation of Turning Point.

David and his wife, Donna, reside in El Cajon, California, where he is the senior pastor of Shadow Mountain Community Church and chancellor of Christian Heritage College. David and Donna have four children and twelve grandchildren.

In 1982, Dr. Jeremiah brought the same solid teaching to San Diego television that he shares weekly with his congregation. Shortly thereafter, Turning Point expanded its ministry to radio. Dr. Jeremiah's inspiring messages can now be heard world wide on radio and television.

Because Dr. Jeremiah desires to know his listening audience, he travels nationwide holding ministry rallies that touch the hearts and lives of many people. According to Dr. Jeremiah, "At some point in time, everyone reaches a turning point; and for every person, that moment is unique, an experience to hold onto forever. There's so much changing in today's world that sometimes it's difficult to choose the right path. Turning Point offers people an understanding of God's Word as well as the opportunity to make a difference in their lives."

Dr. Jeremiah has authored numerous books, including *Escape the Coming Night* (Revelation), *The Handwriting on the Wall* (Daniel), *Overcoming Loneliness, Angels, Prayer—The Great Adventure, God in You* (Holy Spirit), *When Your World Falls Apart, Slaying the Giants in Your Life, My Heart's Desire, Hopeful Parenting, Agents of the Apocalypse, Captured by Grace*, and *God Loves You: He Always Has—He Always Will.*

ABOUT THIS STUDY GUIDE

The purpose of this Turning Point study guide is to reinforce Dr. David Jeremiah's dynamic, in-depth teaching on *Romans* and to aid the reader in applying biblical truth to his or her daily life. We have designed this study guide to correlate with Dr. Jeremiah's *Living by Faith, Volume 3* audio series. It can also stand alone for personal or group Bible study.

STRUCTURE OF THE LESSONS

Each lesson is based on one of the messages in the *Living by Faith, Volume 3* compact disc series and focuses on specific passages from the Bible. Each lesson is composed of the following elements:

- *Outline*

The outline at the beginning of the lesson gives a clear, concise picture of the passage being studied and provides a helpful framework for readers as they listen to Dr. Jeremiah's teaching.

- *Overview*

The overview summarizes Dr. Jeremiah's teaching on the passage being studied in the lesson. Readers should refer to the biblical passages in their own Bibles as they study the overview.

- *Application*

This section contains a variety of questions designed to help readers dig deeper into the lesson and the Scriptures, and to apply the lesson to their daily lives. For Bible study groups or Sunday school classes, these questions will provide a springboard for group discussion and interaction.

- *Did You Know?*

This section presents a fascinating fact, historical note, or insight that adds a point of interest to the preceding lesson.

Using This Guide for Group Study

The lessons in this study guide are suitable for Sunday school classes, small-group studies, elective Bible studies, or home Bible study groups. Each person in the group should have his or her own study guide.

When possible, the study guide should be used with the corresponding compact disc series. You may wish to assign the study guide as homework prior to the meeting of the group and then use the meeting time to listen to the tape and discuss the lesson.

For Continuing Study

For a complete listing of Dr. Jeremiah's materials for personal and group study call 1-800-947-1993, go online to www.DavidJeremiah.org or write to: Turning Point, P.O. Box. 3838, San Diego, CA 92163.

Dr. Jeremiah's *Turning Point* program is currently heard or viewed around the world on radio, television, and the Internet in English. *Momento Decisivo*, the Spanish translation of Dr. Jeremiah's messages, can be heard on radio in every Spanish speaking country in the world. The television broadcast is also broadcast by satellite throughout the Middle East with Arabic subtitles.

Contact Turning Point for radio and television program times and stations in your area. Or visit our website at www.DavidJeremiah.org.

LIVING BY FAITH
VOLUME III

William Wilberforce, the nineteenth century British abolitionist, was a committed Christian. He had been trying to persuade his friend, William Pitt the Younger, prime minister of England, to go with him to hear the great British preacher Richard Cecil. Pitt was a churchgoer, a nominal Christian at best, and Wilberforce felt that sitting under the preaching of the great Cecil might awaken true and saving faith in his friend's heart.

Finally, Pitt agreed to go and hear Cecil preach. The two men sat through a powerfully preached message centered in the truth of God. As the two men left the church, Pitt turned to his friend and said, "You know, Wilberforce, I have not the slightest idea what that man has been talking about." James Boice comments, "Clearly, Pitt was as deaf to God as if he were a physically dead man."[1]

The difference between William Wilberforce and William Pitt is a picture of the dividing line between spiritual life and fleshly life presented in Romans, chapter 8. This chapter of the Bible has been called the greatest chapter in the greatest book containing the greatest verse in all of Scripture (8:28). Whether all of those superlatives are true is perhaps a matter of debate, but this much is certain: No other chapter in all of the Bible presents so clearly what the spiritual life is all about.

In his letter to the Romans Paul has just concluded two chapters in which the insufficiency of man's fleshly nature has been demonstrated. So insufficient is the flesh of man that it had to be positionally put to death when Christ died on the cross (Romans 6). Yet so alive does the flesh remain experientially that it wages war in the inner man of the believer (Romans 7). So what is the solution for the one who wants to live for Christ? Life must be lived in the power of the Holy Spirit (Romans 8): "The law of the Spirit of life in Christ Jesus has made [us] free from the law of sin and death" (8:2).

Paul explains in this great chapter of Scripture how man is utterly powerless to do the right thing in his own fleshly strength. The Law, which was given for our good, fails in our lives because we are not capable of keeping it. Therefore Paul says a change must occur. We must take our minds off trying to find life by keeping the Law and set our minds on the Spirit of life. Only those whose lives are controlled by the Holy Spirit will ultimately be able to live a righteous life. Indeed, Paul says, unless we have the Holy Spirit in us we cannot even consider ourselves children of God.

But those who are God's children enter into an experience which the flesh can never reproduce—adoption as children of God. Becoming co-heirs with God's own Son means that we can call God our own Father—our "Abba" Father. Instead of living life controlled by a spirit of fear, we receive the Spirit of adoption, of sonship. As God's children, we can, for the first time in our lives, relax and rest in the abundance and adequacy of God's provision. But that's only the beginning of the blessing. Paul moves from the truth of our sonship to the trustworthiness of our Savior. The believer in Christ is protected forever in the love of God revealed to us in Christ Jesus.

If William Pitt was unmoved by the words of a great preacher, he would have been doubly confused by Romans, chapter 8. For only spiritual life can respond to spiritual truth. But those who are spiritually alive in Christ will revel in the riches they discover in this "greatest" of Biblical chapters.

Note:

1. James M. Boice, *Romans, An Expositional Commentary,* 4 vols. (Grand Rapids: Baker Book House, 1991, 1992, 1993, 1995), 2:808–809.

A REVOLUTIONARY FREEDOM

Romans 8:1–4

In this lesson we are introduced to true freedom found only in Christ.

OUTLINE

Different people have their own definitions of freedom—freedom from poverty, freedom from tyranny, freedom from authority, freedom from worry and fear. But the most basic freedom of all is freedom from the penalty, power, and practice of sin.

I. **Freedom From the Penalty of Sin**
   A. Sin's Enslavement
   B. Salvation's Emancipation

II. **Freedom From the Power of Sin**
   A. The Law of the Spirit
   B. The Law of Sin and Death

III. **Freedom From the Practice of Sin**

IV. **Freedom for Personal Sanctification**

An old German commentator named Spener said that if the Bible were a ring and the Book of Romans its precious stone, chapter 8 would be "the sparkling point of the jewel."[1]

In Romans chapter 7, we learned about indwelling sin. Now, in chapter 8, we will learn about the indwelling Spirit of God. Chapter 8 is one of the great chapters of the Bible, revealing how the Holy Spirit operates in the believer enabling him to overcome the power of sin.

The first four verses are like an overture to a great symphony— all of the themes of the chapter are revealed. Paul announces that in Christ there is freedom from the penalty, the power, and the practice of sin, and therefore freedom to pursue personal sanctification. No wonder many Christians have memorized this entire chapter!

FREEDOM FROM THE PENALTY OF SIN (8:1)

Charles Trumbull, editor of the old *Sunday School Times*, wrote these words:

> The eighth chapter of Romans has become peculiarly precious to me, beginning with 'no condemnation,' ending with 'no separation,' and in between, 'no defeat.' This wondrous chapter sets forth the gospel and plan of salvation; the life of freedom and victory, the hopelessness of the natural man and the righteousness of the born again; the indwelling of Christ and the Holy Spirit, the resurrection of the body and the blessed hope of Christ's return; the working together of all things for our good; every tense of the Christian life, past, present, and future; and the glorious, climactic song of triumph, no separation in time or eternity 'from the love of God which is in Jesus Christ our Lord.'[2]

Sin's Enslavement

One does not have to read very far into the record of Scripture to discover that sin is a destructive and deadly force.

1. Sin is congenital.

   "Behold, I was brought forth in iniquity, And in sin my mother conceived me" (Psalm 51:5).

2. Sin is universal.

   "For all have sinned and fall short of the glory of God" (Romans 3:23).

3. Sin is natural.

"Among whom also we all once conducted ourselves in the lusts of our flesh, fulfilling the desires of the flesh and of the mind, and were by nature children of wrath, just as the others" (Ephesians 2:3).

4. Sin is familial.

"You do the deeds of your father . . . . You are of your father the devil, and the desires of your father you want to do. He was a murderer from the beginning, and does not stand in the truth . . ." (John 8:41, 44).

5. Sin is fearful.

"But a certain fearful expectation of judgment; and fiery indignation which will devour the adversaries" (Hebrews 10:27).

6. Sin is fatal.

"He who believes and is baptized will be saved: but he who does not believe will be condemned" (Mark 16:16).

"If anyone does not love the Lord Jesus Christ, let him be accursed" (1 Corinthians 16:22).

"In flaming fire taking vengeance on those who do not know God, and on those who do not obey the gospel of our Lord Jesus Christ" (2 Thessalonians 1:8).

In summary, the Bible teaches that all human beings are sinners by birth (sin is congenital; Ephesians 2:3) and sinners by choice (Romans 2:6, 8).

Salvation's Emancipation

There are four key thoughts in Romans 8:1 concerning our freedom from the penalty of sin: Therefore; now; no condemnation; in Christ Jesus.

1. The reason for our emancipation ("therefore")

Paul begins chapter 8 with a "therefore" which indicates a summary—but not just of chapter 7. He is summarizing the entire argument of the epistle up to this point—especially the truth of Romans 5:1. It is interesting to note that the first verses of chapters 5 and 8 are complimentary to each other.

Romans 5:1 is the positive statement: "Therefore, having been justified by faith, we have peace with God through our Lord Jesus Christ."

Romans 8:1 is the negative statement: "There is therefore now no condemnation to those who are in Christ Jesus, who do not walk according to the flesh, but according to the Spirit."

2. The result of our emancipation ("now")

"Now" contrasts the times gone by before we enjoyed emancipation from our sins through the justification brought by Christ. This captures the difference between a believer and an unbeliever: The believer's judgment day is behind him, at the cross of Calvary. The unbeliever's judgment day is ahead of him. Because the believer's judgment day is completed, there is now no condemnation.

3. The reality of our emancipation ("no condemnation")

"Condemnation" is a legal term which includes both the sentence and the execution of the sentence. Charles Cranfield speaks to the removal of the sentence: "For those who are in Christ Jesus . . . there is no divine condemnation, since the condemnation they deserve has already been fully born for them by Him."[3] F. F. Bruce points out the freedom from the effects of the sentence: "There is no reason why those who are in Christ Jesus should go on doing penal servitude as though they had never been pardoned and liberated from the prison house of sin."[4]

4. The relationship of our emancipation ("in Christ Jesus")

Everything we have, according to Paul, is because we are "in Christ Jesus." Martin Luther spoke eloquently of this relationship in one of his writings: "It is impossible for a man to be a Christian without having Christ, and if he has Christ, he has at the same time all that is in Christ. What gives peace to the conscience is that by faith our sins are no more ours, but Christ's upon whom God hath laid them all; and that, on the other hand, all Christ's righteousness is ours, to whom God hath given it. Christ lays His hand upon us, and we are healed. He casts His mantle upon us, and we are clothed; for He is the glorious Savior, blessed for ever . . . . Faith unites the soul with Christ as a spouse with her husband. Everything which Christ has, becomes the property of the believing soul; everything which the soul has, becomes the property of Christ. Christ possesses all blessings and eternal life; they are thenceforward the property of the soul. The soul has all its iniquities and sins:

They become thenceforward the property of Christ. It is then that a blessed exchange commences; Christ who is both God and man, Christ who has never sinned, and whose holiness is perfect, Christ the Almighty and Eternal, taking to Himself, by His nuptial ring of faith, all the sins of the believer, those sins are lost and abolished in Him, for no sins dwell before His infinite righteousness. Thus by faith the believer's soul is delivered from sins and clothed with the eternal righteousness of her bridegroom Christ.[5]

FREEDOM FROM THE POWER OF SIN (8:2)

Paul now sets out to contrast two laws: the Law of Life through the Holy Spirit and the Law of Death through the condemnation of sin.

The Law of the Spirit

The theme of chapter 8 is the Holy Spirit. In Romans 1–7 the Holy Spirit was mentioned only two times: once in a passing reference to "the Spirit of holiness" (1:4) and once in describing how the Holy Spirit pours out God's love in our hearts (5:5). But in chapter 8 the Holy Spirit is referred to no less than 20 times! Second Corinthians 3:17 says, "Where the Spirit of the Lord is, there is freedom," and Romans, chapter 8, is definitely the chapter of freedom through the Spirit of God.

Leon Morris points out,

The Spirit of God is the distinguishing mark of the Christian, and this presence means the defeat of the power of sin . . . . Paul is saying that when the Holy Spirit comes into a person that person is liberated from bondage to evil and finds a new power within, a power that causes the defeat of sin and leads the liberated person into ways of goodness and love.[6]

A summary of the references to the Holy Spirit in chapter 8 reveals the breadth and depth of Paul's emphasis:

8:1 "walking by the Spirit"

8:2 "the law of the Spirit"

8:4 "walking according to the Spirit"

8:5 "living according to the Spirit"

8:5 "the things of the Spirit"

8:6 "spiritually minded"

8:9 "You are not in the flesh but in the Spirit."

8:9 "Indeed the Spirit of God dwells in you."

8:9 "If anyone does not have the Spirit of Christ he is not His."

8:10 "The Spirit is life because of righteousness."

8:11 "The Spirit of Him who raised Jesus ... dwells in you."

8:11 "Will also give life to your mortal bodies through His Spirit who dwells in you."

8:13 "If by the Spirit you put to death the deeds of the body, you will live."

8:14 "For as many as are led by the Spirit of God, these are the sons of God."

8:15 "You have received the Spirit of adoption by whom we cry out Abba Father."

8:16 "The Spirit Himself bears witness with our spirit that we are the children of God."

8:23 "We also who have the firstfruits of the Spirit."

8:26 "Likewise the Spirit also helps in our weaknesses."

8:26 "The Spirit Himself makes intercession for us with groanings which cannot be uttered."

8:27 "He who searches the hearts knows what the mind of the Spirit is."

The Law of Sin and Death

This reference to "the law of sin and death" is to the Law of Moses—the Torah. While that law is not sinful, it condemns sin (Romans 7:7–9). While it does not become death to people, yet it produced death in Paul (7:13).

This passage tells us that the Law of Sin and death keeps the Christian from living the kind of life God wants us to live. The Law of the Spirit of life in Christ Jesus sets us free from the Law of Sin and death. In the same way, the law of gravity acts to keep a plane from flying. But when a plane reaches a certain speed, the law of aerodynamics takes over and frees the plane from the effects of gravitational force.

FREEDOM FROM THE PRACTICE OF SIN (8:3)

A number of key Scriptures from Paul's earlier chapters in Romans, and also from Galatians, provide background for his teaching on freedom from the Law and the condemnation it brings:

"Now we know that whatever the law says, it says to those who are under the law, that every mouth may be stopped, and all the world may become guilty before God" (Romans 3:19).

"Moreover the law entered that the offense might abound. But where sin abounded, grace abounded much more" (Romans 5:20).

"Has then what is good become death to me? Certainly not! But sin, that it might appear sin, was producing death in me through what is good, so that sin through the commandment might become exceedingly sinful" (Romans 7:13).

"For as many as are of the works of the law are under the curse: for it is written. Cursed is everyone who does not continue in all things which are written in the book of the law, to do them . . . . Is the law then against the promise of God? Certainly not! For if there had been a law given which could have given life, truly righteousness would have been by the law" (Galatians 3:10, 21).

"Paul is saying that there is something that the Law of Moses . . . simply could not do, and that God now has done that thing. The reason for the law's failure is that it was 'weak through the flesh.' Consistently Paul sees 'the flesh' not as evil, but as weak—so weak . . . that the law could not bring about salvation."[7]

The problem with the Law is that human weakness robbed it of all its power. The Law is not weak in itself but rather it is weak because of our inability to keep it. So in order to deal with this humanly insurmountable problem, God sent forth His only Son to meet the demands of the law that were rightly leveled against us. Through His Son we are justified freely from all sin. Then God sent forth His Spirit who indwells us and enables us to meet the requirements of God's law in our daily experience.

Paul uses key expressions to describe what God did for us to liberate us from the Law of Sin and Death. Each of these expressions safeguards an important doctrine of the Christian faith. The deity of Christ is set forth when Paul says God sent forth His own Son. And the incarnation of Christ is affirmed when he says Christ came in the likeness of sinful flesh. John Stott describes the exactness of Paul's expression: "Not 'in sinful flesh', because the flesh of Jesus was sinless. Nor 'in the likeness of flesh,' because the flesh of Jesus was both sinless and real."[8]

Finally, the substitutionary atonement of Christ is affirmed by Paul when he says Christ came on account of sin. Sin was the reason Jesus came to earth, to condemn sin in the flesh. Leon Morris points out that "Paul is now picturing sin as a litigant in a law court; the verdict goes against sin and thus sin is condemned . . . . There is the thought that the condemnation is brought into effect (as when a . . . building is 'condemned'; it is used no more, and demolition follows)."[9]

FREEDOM FOR PERSONAL SANCTIFICATION (8:4)

Kent Hughes summarizes the meaning of verse 4:

[Christ] condemned sin in his flesh 'in order that the righteous requirements of the law might be fully met in us, who do not live according to the sinful nature but according to the Spirit.' The Holy Spirit creates a new humanity which is characterized by walking 'according to the Spirit.' This new humanity, through its union with Christ, whose flesh never sinned, is infused with the power to live in a way that is pleasing to God. Everything the Law required is now realized in the lives of those who are controlled by the Holy Spirit.[10]

Leon Morris continues,

God's commands have now become God's enablings . . . . In the full sense, only Christ has fulfilled all the law's requirements, but when we are in him we in our measure begin to live the kind of life that God would have us live . . . . Before we came to know Christ we were continually defeated by sin. When we came to know him and to receive the indwelling Holy Spirit, we were able to attain a standard we could never reach in our own strength.[11]

The believer has been given four new realities in Christ Jesus:

1. A New Position - "We are in Christ."
2. A New Peace - "No condemnation."
3. A New Power - "The Spirit of life in Christ Jesus."
4. A New Potential - "The righteous requirements of the law may be fulfilled in us."

Notes:

1. Godet, *Commentary on St. Paul's Epistle to the Romans,* Vol. 2, 57.

2. Quoted by Donald Grey Barnhouse, *Epistle to the Romans,* part 1 of the printed radio messages (Philadelphia: The Bible Study Hour, 1953), 1982.

3. C. E. B. Cranfield, *A Critical and Exegetical Commentary on the Epistle to the Romans* (Edinburgh: T & T Clark, 1975), 373.

4. F. F. Bruce, *The Epistle of Paul To The Romans* (London: The Tyndale Press, 1966), 151.

5. Cited by Robert Haldane, *Exposition of the Epistle To The Romans* (MacDill AFB: MacDonald Publishing, 1958), 312–3.

6. Leon Morris, *The Epistle to the Romans* (Grand Rapids: InterVarsity Press, 1994), 300.

7. Leon Morris, 302.

8. John Stott, *Romans: God's Good News For The World* (Downer's Grove, IL: InterVarsity Press, 1994), 219.

9. Leon Morris, 303.

10. Kent Hughes, *Romans - Righteousness From Heaven* (Wheaton: Crossway Books, 1991), 150.

11. Leon Morris, 304.

APPLICATION

1. Read John 3:5–8.

   a. What two things are required for a person to be able to see the kingdom of God? (verse 5)

   b. What do you think the reference to "water" means in verse 5?

   c. What are the two distinct categories of existence which apply to every person? (verse 6)

   d. How many "births" must every person experience in order to see the kingdom of God?

   e. Why did Jesus say that Nicodemus shouldn't have been surprised at the requirement to be born a second time? (verse 7; see verse 10)

f. How is the Holy Spirit to be compared to the wind? (verse 8)

g. How do you know the wind is present?

h. How do you know whether a person has born again by the Spirit? (verse 8)

2. Read Titus 3:3–7.

   a. Before one is born again by the Holy Spirit, (to one degree or another) what characterizes his or her life? (verse 3)

   b. In light of the descriptions in verse 3, how would you define the "mercy" that saved us? (verse 5)

c. What is Jesus Christ called in verse 4?

d. How was God's mercy exercised towards us? (verse 5b)

e. How does the "washing" of the Holy Spirit in verse 5 relate to being born of "water" in John 3:5?

f. What is the connection between those who are saved and those who are washed, re-born, and renewed through the Holy Spirit? Is a person saved who has not been born again by the Spirit?

3. Read Romans 7:7–13.

a. What is Paul's answer to the question, "Is the law sin?" (verse 7)

b. What, in verse 6, might have prompted the question in verse 7?

c. What does the Law do in us? (verse 7)

d. What does our sinful nature do with what the Law reveals? (verse 8)

e. How could the Law ever have originally brought life? (verse 10; Leviticus 18:5; Deuteronomy 30:8, 10–11, 15–16, 19)

f. How did sin bring death? (verses 10–11)

g. So which is evil—the Law or our sin nature?

h. What was the ultimate purpose of God's giving of the Law? (verse 13)

4. What exchange does Paul describe in 2 Corinthians 5:21 that allowed us to go free from the condemnation of the Law?

5. Like trees moving in the wind, list the signs which should accompany the life of a person upon whom the Spirit has moved for salvation? (Galatians 5:22–23)

DID YOU KNOW?

When Jesus was talking to Nicodemus about the necessity for new birth by the Spirit, He was also talking to you. The word "you" is mentioned twice in John 3:7: "Do not marvel that I said to you, 'You must be born again.'" The first "you" is singular in Greek—referring to Nicodemus—but the second "you" is plural, referring to everyone. Nicodemus, as a leading teacher in Israel, was shocked when Jesus said that "you all (in Israel)" need to be born again (John 3:9). If you are shocked or offended at Jesus' suggestion that *you* need to be born again, don't be. It's the only way to ever see the kingdom of God.

THE SPIRIT AND THE FLESH

Romans 8:5–11

In this lesson we discover the stark contrast between two kinds of human beings.

OUTLINE

In a day when tolerance and non-discrimination are cultural watchwords, we must not forget that God still discriminates. He draws a firm line between spiritually-minded and carnally-minded persons. For that reason, it's a good idea to know which is which.

I. **There Are Two Divisions Among Men**
   A. Those Who Live According to the Flesh
   B. Those Who Live According to the Spirit

II. **There Are Two Dispositions Among Men**
   A. The Fleshly Mind-Set
   B. The Spiritual Mind-Set

III. **There Are Two Destinies Among Men**
   A. The Destiny of the Carnally Minded
   B. The Destiny of the Spiritually Minded

IV. **There Are Two Dominions Over Men**
   A. The Dominion of the Flesh
   B. The Dominion of the Spirit

As we have already learned, Romans 7 is dominated by the words "I," "me," and "my." In contrast, Romans 8 is dominated by the Holy Spirit, who is mentioned by name 19 times in this chapter. Paul reveals that the Holy Spirit changes our nature and grants us strength for victory over our unredeemed flesh.

Throughout the epistle, Paul has relied on contrasts to get his point across: Adam and Christ, slavery and freedom, death and life—and now he pits the flesh and the Spirit against each other.

THERE ARE TWO DIVISIONS AMONG MEN

In God's eyes, there are only two kinds of people in the world—those who live according to the flesh and those who live according to the Spirit. As John MacArthur points out: "As far as spiritual life is concerned, God takes no consideration of gender, age, education, talent, class, race, or any other human distinctions (Galations 3:28). He differentiates people solely on the basis of their relationship to Him, and the difference is absolute."[1]

Donald Grey Barnhouse devotes a whole chapter in his book on Romans to explain that there are only two kinds of men. As he introduces that chapter, here is some of what he says:

> According to the Word of God, there are only two kinds of people in the world, those who have been born once and those who have been born twice. God will never divide people into what the world calls educated or uneducated, cultured or savage, religious or irreligious, rich or poor, high or low, noble or ignoble. Our present text shows that the only difference God recognizes is that between the men who do not have divine life and those who do. There are those who are after the flesh, and those who are after the Spirit . . . . Two different persons may be active in a parent-teacher association, yet the activity of the one may be according to the flesh, and the activity of the other may be according to the Spirit. Two women may keep their homes spotless, yet the one may do it according to the flesh and the other according to the Spirit. Two people may do church work, yet the one may do it according to the flesh and the other according to the Spirit.[2]

Those Who Live According to the Flesh

A good concordance will reveal . . . a long list of things that are connected with the flesh, all of which are hateful to God: the affections of the flesh, confidence in the flesh, the deeds of the flesh, the desires of the flesh, the faith of the flesh, the religion of the flesh, the prayers of the flesh, the worship according to the flesh, the god of the flesh. When we put all these things together we have a picture of the normal, natural man, untouched by the Spirit of God . . . . The acts of the unsaved man proceed from the thoughts of his flesh; they are all alien to the life of God, and therefore cannot please God. The unsaved man lives for self, even though he is giving his life for the service of others.[3]

Those Who Live According to the Spirit

The rest of this lesson is an exposition of the quality of life that belongs to those who live according to the Spirit.

THERE ARE TWO DISPOSITIONS AMONG MEN (8:5)

In Romans 8:5, Paul's term, "set their minds," is the Greek word *phroneo*. It refers to the basic orientation, bent, or thought patterns of the mind. It is the sum total of our inner dispositions which influence and determine our behavior and lifestyle. It is what motivates our outlook, our assumptions, our values, our desires, and our goals, whether consciously or unconsciously. It is what we are most deeply interested in and what we constantly talk about.

The Fleshly Mind-Set

Those whose mind-set is after the flesh indulge the flesh in its corrupt desires. This does not mean they are living a gross, vicious life. The flesh may be educated, refined and cultured. "Flesh" minus the "h" spelled backwards is "self."

Haldane describes vividly the man with the fleshly mind-set:

Such persons have their minds intent on the things that gratify their corrupt nature. They have no relish for spiritual things; whatever they may be induced to do from dread of punishment, or hope of reward in a future world, their desires are, in reality, centered in the things of this world. Whatever may be their profession of religion, their hearts are supremely engrossed with earthly things . . . in one word, they mind the things of the flesh, they love the world and all that is in the world.[4]

The Spiritual Mind-Set

Those who live according to the Spirit set their minds on godly things. Even when believers falter in their obedience to Christ, their orientation does not change.

As Paul asserted in Romans 7, the Christian still battles with the flesh because his body, not yet redeemed, tries to lure him back into his old sinful ways. But he is no longer in the flesh but in the Spirit. Therefore, "If we live in the Spirit, let us also walk in the Spirit" (Galatians 5:25). Since a believer's nature is divine, he should desire to behave accordingly.

Kent Hughes summarizes Paul's point:

What Paul is saying here is immensely important because our mind-set makes all the difference when it comes to daily living. We all, whatever our spiritual state, live in a storm-tossed world. The rain falls on the just and the unjust. The set of our minds will determine not only eternity but the quality of our life now.[5]

THERE ARE TWO DESTINIES AMONG MEN (8:6)

The contrast between the Spirit and flesh reaches a climax in verse 6. Here we learn that a disposition controlled by sin not only leads to ultimate death, it is death even now. And a disposition controlled by the Spirit is life and peace even now as well as for eternity.

The Destiny of the Carnally Minded

1. The carnal mind is characterized by hostility toward God

Earlier (Romans 5:10) Paul mentioned that apart from Christ we are God's enemies. Sin and holiness are at enmity with one another. "How readily we assume that, left to itself, human nature is basically good, or if not good, at least neutral. Not so, according to Paul. Human egotism is fiercely hostile to God. It honors the made above the Maker, serves self before others, loves self rather than God. Left to itself, human nature is not a domesticated animal; it is like a wild beast—locked in mortal combat against Christ. Whether its expressions are socially acceptable or not does not change its fundamental hostility to God and its ultimate destructiveness."[6]

There are countless examples in Scripture of the . . . enmity of the carnal mind. Think of Abraham marrying Hagar; Lot choosing Sodom; Moses smiting the Egyptian; Joshua making a deal with the Gibeonites; Saul sparing the Amalekite cattle; Solomon's political marriages; Jonah fleeing to Tarshish; Peter smiting Malchus. These and many others illustrate the principle. There is only one way to avoid the mistakes made by the carnal mind and that is to have the mind of Christ (Philippians 2:5; 1 Corinthians 2:16). The only way to have the mind of Christ is to allow the Spirit of Christ to control the mind.[7]

Leon Morris explains the far-reaching effect of this condition of hostility:

It is not simply being slightly uncooperative; it is downright hostility. It means being in the opposite camp, refusing to be subject to God's law . . . . The implication is that [the mind] ought to submit to God's law. But the person whose general bent is towards the things of this earth, fleshly things, the person contaminated by his fallenness, is by that very fact rebellious against God's law . . . . Indeed . . . such a mind cannot submit t o God . . . . There is no possibility that anyone will at the same time set the course of his life on the merely fleshly and be obedient to God.[8]

2. The carnal mind is characterized by death

While the carnal man may have physical life, he is dead spiritually. His values, priorities, and concerns are those of this world only—a world which is passing away (Proverbs 14:23; 16:24; Matthew 7:13–14; Romans 6:21; 1 John 2:15–17).

The Destiny of the Spiritually Minded

1. The spiritual mind is characterized by peace

William Hendrickson describes this special peace:
". . . the inner assurance that past sins are forgiven, that present events, no matter how painful, are being over-ruled for good, and that nothing that might occur in the future will be able to separate him from the love of God in Christ. Such peace means basic freedom from fear and from restlessness. It implies contentment, a sense of security, inner tranquility."[9]

Scripture is filled with abundant testimony of the peace that comes to the spiritually-minded person:

• Psalm 4:8 - "I will both lie down in peace, and sleep; For you alone, O Lord, make me dwell in safety."

- John 14:27 - 'Peace I leave with you. My peace I give to you, not as the world gives do I give to you. Let not your heart be troubled, neither let it be afraid."

2. The spiritual mind is characterized by life

   Only those who have experienced new life in Christ, the life produced by the Spirit, know that life without Christ is not really life at all. The life Jesus Christ came to give is the abundant life experienced by those who have a spiritual mind-set produced by the Spirit:

   - John 17:3 - "And this is eternal life, that they may know You, the only true God, and Jesus Christ whom You have sent."
   - John 10:10 - "I have come that they might have life and that they might have it more abundantly."
   - 1 John 1:2 - "The life was manifested, and we have seen, and bear witness, and declare to you that eternal life which was with the Father and was manifested to us."

THERE ARE TWO DOMINIONS OVER MEN (8:8-11)

There is a progression in the way Paul describes both categories of people. They are first of all "according to" (8:4–5) and now they are "in." The terms move from the pattern of one's life to the sphere of one's life.

The Dominion of the Flesh

The primary characteristic of being in the flesh is our absolute inability to please God (8:8). Only surrender to the Holy Spirit can guarantee that our motives will be pleasing to God since the heart of man is deceitful and desperately wicked (Jeremiah 17:9–10).

The Dominion of the Spirit

Beginning with verse 9, Paul shifts from the third person to the second person and addresses his readers personally, exhorting them to acknowledge the Spirit in their lives.

1. The Holy Spirit inhabits every believer.

   The acid test of one's faith is the indwelling presence of the Holy Spirit (8:9). Paul says that you can be certain of your salvation if indeed the Spirit of God dwells in you. The word for "dwell" in the Greek language is a word that means "to be at home with" or "to be in one's own home." The Spirit is not an occasional visitor; he takes up residence in God's people.

2. The Holy Spirit invigorates every believer.

   Paul does not deny the effect of the fallen nature upon us. Our bodies carry within them the fatal flaw of sin. But there is another more powerful agent at work within them also— the Spirit of Life. While outwardly it may appear as if sin is having its decaying effect, there is another force at work. This is pictured by three contrasts in verse 10: The body is contrasted with the soul; death is contrasted with life; sin is contrasted with righteousness.

3. The Holy Spirit insures every believer.

   In verse 11, "Without denying the sober grip of sin in the life of the Christian, Paul encourages the Romans. God counts them under the authority of the Spirit even though the Spirit's work is not yet completed."[10]

The words "mortal" and "immortal" always refer to the body. The body is still subject to death in the ordinary course of events because of sin. The human spirit has been made alive by the Holy Spirit at the time of regeneration. At the time of the Resurrection these bodies of ours will be clothed with life immortal, too (Romans 8:22–23; 13:11; 1 Corinthians 15:42–44).

In this section of Romans, we are brought face to face with the priority of the Holy Spirit in the life of the believer. Three titles are given to the Holy Spirit. He is the "Spirit of God" (8:9), the "Spirit of Christ" (8:10), and "the Spirit of Him who raised Jesus from the dead" (8:11).

We are reminded that even though we have been redeemed from the power of the flesh, we can still live fleshly lives if we do not yield to the power of the Holy Spirit. We must let Him control our lives or we will fall back into the old patterns of sin and the flesh. Three principles from this lesson can make the difference in the believer living a victorious, or a defeated, Christian life:

1. The Holy Spirit is the believer's help.

   Twice we are told in this passage that the Holy Spirit dwells in us as believers (8:9, 11). When the believer allows the Holy Spirit to control him, he has the power to live a holy life.

2. The Holy Spirit is the believer's holiness.

   In this section of Romans we are told that we are to live "according to the Spirit" and to let the Spirit control us. When this happens and our whole inner being is turned definitely and constantly in the direction of the Holy Spirit, purity becomes our very life. Remember, He is the *Holy* Spirit.

3. The Holy Spirit is the believer's hope.

   In this passage, the indwelling Holy Spirit is associated with our future resurrection. He is the seal that God has given to every believer that he shall live forever in the presence of the Father.

On June 12, 1979, a young man made aviation history when he flew a pedal-powered plane across the English Channel. Taking off from England, he flew for three hours, rarely more than 15 feet above the water. Finally, after covering 22 miles, he landed exhausted on the coast of France. As dramatic as this was, man-powered flight will never be practical. A man simply cannot maintain the necessary energy output for extended flights.

In the same way, no one can live the Christian life on his or her own power. It is only through the enabling power of the Holy Spirit that we can consistently live the Christian life.

Notes:

1. John MacArthur, *The MacArthur New Testament Commentary - Romans 1–8* (Chicago: Moody Press, 1991), 416.

2. Donald Grey Barnhouse, *God's Grace—God's Freedom* - Romans Vol. III (Grand Rapids: Wm. B. Eerdmans, 1953), 23–4, 27.

3. Barnhouse, 24–25.

4. Robert Haldane, *Exposition of the Epistle To The Romans* (MacDill AFB: MacDonald Publishing, 1958), 331.

5. Ken Hughes, *Romans—Righteousness from Heaven* (Wheaton: Crossway Books, 1991), 151.

6. Notes on Romans - Lesson 15 - *Community Bible Study* (MacLean: VA, 1983–4), 6.

7. John Phillips, *Exploring Romans* (Chicago: Moody Press, 1969), p. 125.

8. Leon Morris, *The Epistle To The Romans* (Grand Rapids: InterVarsity Press, 1994), 306.

9. William Hendriksen, *New Testament Commentary - Exposition of Paul's Epistle To The Romans* (Grand Rapids: Baker Books, 1980–1), 249.

10. *Community Bible Study,* 6.

1. What do the following verses tell you about "setting your mind" on spiritual things?

   a. Romans 12:16. What does it mean to set your mind on "high things?"

   b. Why is being wise "in your opinion" a temptation not to stay spiritually minded? Philippians 2:5. How do you have the same mind that was in Christ Jesus?

   c. How do you know when you are letting the mind of the flesh characterize you instead of the mind of Christ?

   d. Colossians 3:2. Name three ways that you can set your mind on things above:

e. Name three indications that you have your mind set on things of this world:

f. What is the greatest temptation for you to take your mind off heavenly things?

g. Matthew 16:23. What was Peter doing that indicated he was not mindful of the things of God?

h. What would Peter have done or said in that situation if his mind had been on the things of God instead of the things of men?

i. How would you describe the "things of men" in general terms?

2. How does Peter describe those who walk "according to the flesh?" (2 Peter 2:10)

    a. What does it mean that a person's "god is [his] belly?" (Philippians 3:19)

    b. Name as many different kinds of human appetites (in addition to food) that people have?

    c. If a person's life is driven only by the appetites of the flesh, how would his or her life be characterized?

    d. What would a person "hunger for" whose appetites were of a spiritual instead of an earthly nature?

e. What is your strongest heavenly appetite? Your strongest earthly appetite?

f. What does it mean to be "in the world" but not "of the world?" (1 John 2:15–17)

g. How does Matthew 6:24 relate to 1 John 2:15?

h. Of the three things John warns against in verse 16, which do you struggle with the most?

i. Based on the long-term view of life, why is it foolish to lust after worldly things? (verse 17)

j. Why is it wise to seek after heavenly things?

3. What do the following verses teach about how to please God?
   a. Hebrews 11:6

   b. Romans 12:1–2

   c. 2 Corinthians 5:9

   d. 1 Thessalonians 4:1

4. What insight do you gain about the Holy Spirit in the life of the believer from the following verses?

a. 1 Corinthians 12:13

b. 2 Corinthians 4:16

DID YOU KNOW?

Many new Christians are shocked to discover that life as a believer has more challenges and temptations than life as a non-believer. It's because where there was only the carnal nature present before, now there are two natures which are strident in their opposition to one another. The believer is caught between two opposing forces. Galatians 5:17 says they are "contrary (*antikeimai*, lying against, opposed to) to one another." But to prove how real the battle is, the same Greek word is used of the way the Anti-Christ will one day rise up and oppose the true God (2 Thessalonians 2:4). This is a serious kind of conflict, and every believer should be aware of, and prepared for, the battle between flesh and Spirit.

THE MINISTRY OF THE HOLY SPIRIT

Romans 8:12–17

*In this lesson we discover the blessings
brought to the believer by the Holy Spirit.*

OUTLINE

We are not born again by the Spirit and then abandoned by the
Spirit. We are not released from bondage to the flesh and then
left to struggle on our own. Rather, we are ushered by the Spirit
into an entirely new household of faith—of which God himself
is the Father.

I. **The Believer Is Responsible to the Holy Spirit**

II. **The Believer Is Reinforced by the Holy Spirit**

III. **The Believer Is Ruled by the Holy Spirit**
   A. Leading in Godliness
   B. Leading in General

IV. **The Believer Is Released by the Holy Spirit**
   A. Adoption
   B. Abba Father

V. **The Believer Is Reassured by the Holy Spirit**

VI. **The Believer Is Rewarded by the Holy Spirit**

Romans 8:1–11 reveals how the believer is delivered from the penalty, power, and practice of his sinful flesh. True to form, beginning in verse 12, Paul now takes up the believer's responsibilities in light of the benefits and privileges he has just described. Doctrine first, then duty; exposition, then exhortation.

The believer who has been delivered from the obligation to obey the dictates of the sinful human nature must live in obedience to the Holy Spirit. He becomes obligated to live "after the Spirit" (8:4–5). He is obligated to live in a new way even though he is totally incapable of it in his own strength. Only by the Spirit of God can we fulfill our obligation to walk free from sin. Inherent in our obligation is one of the seeming paradoxes of Scripture. We are called to action, yet we are powerless to act! It is this tension, this attitude of dependence upon God, which Paul presents in Philippians 2:12–13: ". . . work out your own salvation with fear and trembling; for it is God who works in you both to will and to do for His good pleasure."

THE BELIEVER IS RESPONSIBLE TO THE HOLY SPIRIT (8:12)

In the first chapter of Romans, Paul reminds us that we are debtors to share the gospel with the world (1:14). Here he reminds us that we are debtors to live a righteous life. We are not debtors to the flesh—it has done nothing good for us at all. Since the Holy Spirit has given life to our souls and will someday also give eternal life to our mortal bodies, we are responsible to live according to the Spirit and not according to the flesh.

Because we have been made alive (8:10), we must live according to that which gave us life—the Spirit. To live according to the flesh is to live with blinders on—all we can see are the affairs and concerns of this life. Rather than being truly alive, living according to the flesh is to remain in the process of a slow death (1 Timothy 5:6).

THE BELIEVER IS REINFORCED BY THE HOLY SPIRIT (8:13)

The automatic outcome of living according to the flesh is death. But if, by the Holy Spirit's power, we "put to death" the deeds of the body, the automatic outcome is life. John Stott says, "There is a kind of life which leads to death, and there is a kind of death which leads to life."[1] We cannot destroy the flesh in this life, but we can destroy the deeds of the flesh. Though we are no longer in the flesh, the flesh is still in us. Stiffler explains: "The man in Christ is not in the flesh, but it is in him, and the problem of salvation is not how to transmute the flesh into something good, but how to live with this thing every day without being overcome by it. The presence of the Spirit solves the problem."[2]

We are responsible, with the aid of the Holy Spirit, to put to death the misdeeds of the body. After reminding us that this "putting to death" is neither masochism nor asceticism, John Stott describes it like this:

> It is . . . a clear-sighted recognition of evil as evil, leading to such a decisive and radical repudiation of it that no imagery can do it justice except 'putting to death.' In fact, the verb Paul uses normally means to 'kill someone, hand someone over to be killed, especially of the death sentence and its execution . . . .'[3]

The Roman sentence of crucifixion lends insight into the nature of how we must put to death the deeds of the flesh. First, crucifixion was personal, focused on an individual. We must put to death the deeds of our own flesh by walking in the power of the Holy Spirit. Second, crucifixion was painful. We fool ourselves if we think the habits and desires of the flesh will die without a struggle. They will not. Third, crucifixion is pitiless—there is no turning back once the process begins. Victims of crucifixion were not removed from the cross until they were dead. We must be just as merciless in putting to death the deeds of our flesh.

There is good news—on the other side of the death experience is new life! The painful process of crucifying the flesh produces a quality of life not experienced any other way.

THE BELIEVER IS RULED BY THE HOLY SPIRIT (8:14)

More than just reinforcing our new spiritual desires, the Holy Spirit actually leads and guides us toward holiness. The process of being led, and following the Spirit's leadership, is proof positive that we are indeed the children of God. The Spirit leads us in two ways.

Leading in Godliness

First, He leads us to put to death the misdeeds of the body, as Cranfield has said: "The daily, hourly putting to death of the schemings and enterprises of the sinful flesh by means of the Spirit is a matter of being led, directed, impelled, controlled by the Spirit."[4] Though we are being led, we are still responsible to follow proactively. The great theologian Warfield summarizes it eloquently:

> Though it is indeed the Holy Spirit who keeps us in the path and brings us at last to the goal, it is we who tread every step of the way; our limbs that grow weary with the labor, our hearts that faint, . . . our faith that revives our sinking strength; our hope that instills new courage into our souls, as we toil over the steep ascent.[5]

Leading in General

While leading us into sanctification and holiness is the priority, the Holy Spirit leads us in all things as we progress through the Christian life. Paul uses the present tense—"are led"—in verse 14 as a way to characterize the believer's experience of following the Spirit's leading moment by moment. Many believers have laid claim to Proverbs 3:5–6 as their life verse because it speaks of our dependence upon God's leading in everything:

> "Trust in the Lord with all your heart, and lean not on your own understanding; In all your ways acknowledge Him, and He shall direct your paths" (Proverbs 3:5–6).

THE BELIEVER IS RELEASED BY THE HOLY SPIRIT (8:15)

According to verse 15, we have been released from the spirit of fear by the Holy Spirit who has placed us in the body of Christ. We have received the Spirit of adoption. While the actual adoption itself will occur at a future time (8:23) the spirit of adoption provides for every believer release from the bondage that he once knew. The picture that Paul uses is the contrast between slavery and sonship. Slavery, with its fear and isolation, stands for our old lives before knowing Christ. We are told by the writer of Hebrews that Christ died that He might destroy the one who had the power of death and release those who were subject to a fear of death (Hebrews 2:14–15). The perfect love of God has cast out the fear to which we were once enslaved (2 Timothy 1:7; 1 John 4:18).

Anything that involves a believer in fear or bondage cannot possibly be the work of the Holy Spirit of God. It must come either from his own heart of unbelief or as a temptation of the Evil One. Our sonship implies perfect spiritual liberty and the absence of all legal features which would bring us once more 'under law.' It is the work of the Holy Spirit to lead the believer into a position of filial confidence . . . .[6]

Two things confirm that we have been released from fear into sonship: adoption and our ability to call God "Father."

Adoption

The Greek word *huiothesia* (adoption) means to be installed or placed as a son. In Biblical times, it was the legal procedure whereby a person was taken from one family (or no family) and placed into a new family. We have been taken from the family of Adam and placed into the family of God.

When the Christian is 'born again,' his filial relationship to the family of God is bestowed upon him in adoption. There is only one Son of God who is in essence God. But many are made sons through adoption (1 John 1:12). Note that Paul speaks of the 'spirit of adoption,' which is the believer's present possession; whereas the actual act of reception into God's heavenly family awaits the redemption of the body at the revelation of Christ (v. 23).[7]

F. F. Bruce provides these thoughts on adoption:

The term adoption may have a somewhat artificial sound in our ears; but in the Roman world of the first century A.D. an adopted son was a son deliberately chosen by his adoptive father to perpetuate his name and inherit his estate; he was no whit inferior in status to a son born in the ordinary course of nature, and might well enjoy the father's affection more fully and reproduce the father's character more worthily.[8]

Abba Father

Calling God "Abba" is rooted in Jesus agony in the Garden of Gethsemane:

"And He said, 'Abba, Father, all things are possible for You. Take this cup away from Me; nevertheless, not what I will, but what You will'" (Mark 14:36).

Abba was an ordinary family word of Jesus day. It conveyed intimacy, tenderness, dependence, and complete lack of fear or anxiety. Modern English equivalents would be Daddy or Papa.

In other words, ". . . an everyday infant sound is applied without inhibition to God . . . . This basic word tells us that God is not a distant Ruler in transcendence but One who is intimately close."[9]

No Jew would have dreamed of using this very intimate term to address God. However, Jesus always used this word in His prayers (Aramaic *abba* or its Greek equivalent *pater*), with the exception of His cry from the cross. And Jesus instructed His disciples to use this word in their prayers as well. We are empowered to speak to God just as a small child speaks to His father.

THE BELIEVER IS REASSURED BY THE HOLY SPIRIT (8:16)

Paul is not saying that the Holy Spirit bears witness *to* my spirit that I am a child of God, but rather that the Holy Spirit bears witness *with* my spirit that I am a child of God. In other words, at the same time that I am praying and calling God my Father from within my spirit, the Holy Spirit is doing the same thing from within me so that there are two who call God Father every time I pray—the Holy Sprit and my spirit (Galatians 4:6). It is a dual evidence of my sonship. My sonship does not rest for affirmation upon my spirit alone with all of its ups and downs. My sonship rests for affirmation on the unchanging testimony of the Holy Spirit of God who lives within me.

The nineteenth-century British pastor Billy Bray seemed never to have lacked that inner testimony. He had been converted from a life of drunken debauchery while reading John Bunyan's *Visions of Heaven and Hell.* He was so continuously overjoyed by God's grace and goodness that he said, 'I can't help praising the Lord. As I go along the street, I lift up one foot, and it seems to say, 'Glory.' And I lift up the other, and it seems to say, 'Amen.' And so they keep on like that all the time I am walking.'[10]

THE BELIEVER IS REWARDED BY THE HOLY SPIRIT (8:17)

There are three words which describe the rewards of sonship brought by the Holy Spirit. First, we are children. All of the truth about adoption is given here to help us understand our new position as sons instead of slaves. We have been placed as full-grown sons, as adult members of the family. The evidence of our sonship is that we are being led by the Holy Spirit; that we are consciously responsive to His teaching and guidance. And because we are sons, we no longer fear the Father but we come to him boldly, in intimate conversation, addressing him as Abba just as Christ did while on earth. Through the ministry of the Holy Spirit in our hearts, we have been rewarded with sonship.

Second, we are heirs. In ordinary usage, an heir is one who has not yet received his inheritance but is anticipating it sometime in the future. The Biblical idea of "heir" implies actual possession in part here and now, with the promise of complete possession and enjoyment in the future. This goes beyond being a child or even a son. We actually possess in Christ everything that God has for us as Paul says in Colossians 3:23–24: "And whatever you do, do it heartily, as to the Lord and not to men, knowing that from the Lord you will receive the reward of the inheritance; for you serve the Lord Christ."

Third, Paul says we are joint-heirs with Christ. Donald Grey Barnhouse explains the difference between an heir and a joint-heir:

> If a man dies, leaving a large farm to four heirs, the estate is divided evenly and each heir receives twenty-five per cent of the whole. But if a man leaves a farm to four of his sons as joint-heirs, then each son owns the whole farm. Each one can say, 'This house is mine; those barns are mine; those fields are mine.' . . . Thus when the Lord tells us that we are heirs of God and joint-heirs of Jesus Christ, we are being informed that everything that God the Father has given to the Lord Jesus Christ has been given to us also.[11]

> Now the value of an inheritance is determined by the worth of the one who bequeaths it, and the inheritance of Christians is from the Creator, Sustainer, and Owner of the world. God not only is the source of our inheritance but is himself our inheritance. Of all the good things in the universe, the most precious is the Creator of the universe himself. The Psalmist declared, 'Whom have I in heaven but Thee? And besides Thee, I desire nothing on earth.' (Psalm 73:25).[12]

Robert Haldane expresses it beautifully:

> God is the portion of his people, and in him, who is 'the possessor of heaven and earth,' they are heirs of all things . . . . God is all-sufficient, and this is an all-sufficient inheritance. God is eternal and therefore it is an eternal inheritance—an inheritance incorruptible, undefiled and that fadeth not away. . . . It is God himself, then who is the inheritance of his children."[13]

Since God is our inheritance, nothing can keep us from it. Paul mentions that in the process of gaining our inheritance, we will learn something about suffering. Since we are joint-heirs with Christ, and He suffered, we might expect to experience suffering as well. That is the focus of our next lesson.

Notes:

1. John Stott, *Romans: God's Good News For The World*, (Downers Grove: Crossway Books, 1991), 228.

2. James M. Stiffler, *The Epistle To The Romans*, (Chicago: Moody Press, 1960), 148.

3. John Stott, 228.

4. C. E. B. Cranfield, *A Critical and Exegetical Commentary on the Epistle to the Romans*, (Edinburgh; T & T Clark, 1975), 395.

5. Benjamin Warfield, quoted by William Hendriksen, *New Testament Commentary-Exposition of Paul's Epistle To The Romans*, (Grand Rapids: Baker Books, 1980–81), 257.

6. John Phillips, *Exploring Romans*, (Chicago: Moody Press, 1969), 215.

7. *The Criswell Believer's Study Bible*, (Nashville: Thomas Nelson Publishers, 1991) , 1610.

8. F. F. Bruce, *The Epistle of Paul to the Romans*, (London: The Tyndale Press, 1966), 157; [cited by?] William Barclay, *The Letter To The Romans*, (The Saint Andrew Press, 1969), 106.

9. Leon Morris, *The Epistle To The Romans* (Grand Rapids: William B. Eerdmans, 1988), 316.

10. Quoted by John MacArthur, *The MacArthur New Testament Commentary - Romans 1–8*, (Chicago: Moody Press, 1991), 438.

11. Donald Grey Barnhouse, *Romans, God's Heirs - Romans 8:1–39*, (Grand Rapids: Wm B. Eerdman's Publishing Co., 1959), 113.

12. John MacArthur, 444.

13. Robert Haldane, *An Exposition of the Epistle To The Romans*, (MacDill AFB: MacDonald Publishing, 1958), 365.

1. What qualifies a person to be dead at the same time he or she is physically alive? (1 Timothy 5:6)

   a. What does it mean to "live in pleasure?"

   b. With what does Paul contrast that lifestyle? (1 Timothy 5:5)

   c. How do would you interpret verse 5 practically speaking? Is the Godly person one who spends all of their time praying? (see 1 Thessalonians 5:17)

2. Read Galatians 5:16–26.

   a. What contrast does Paul set forth to open this passage? (verse 16)

b. When you do something you know you don't want to do, what is that a sign of? (verse 17)

c. List all the works of the flesh Paul mentions in verses 19–21:

d. In the list above, underline the works of the flesh which were true of you before you became a Christian but which you no longer practice.

e. Now, circle the works of the flesh with which you still struggle to maintain victory in the Spirit.

f. Describe your struggle with these works of the flesh. That is, are you gaining victory? How are you seeking victory? How do you handle defeat?

g. What does Paul say about those who practice the works of the flesh? (verse 21)

h. How does this apply to Christians who may still fail to walk in the Spirit but who have also been promised eternal life?

i. List the fruit of the Spirit Paul mentions in verses 22–23:

j. In the list above, underline the fruit of the Spirit which were not present in your life as a non-Christian but which the Holy Spirit has produced in you.

k. Now, circle the areas in which you desire to give the Holy Spirit even greater control.

l. What is Paul's concluding summary statement? (verse 25)

3. Read Romans 13:11–14.

   a. What is the overall message Paul is delivering in this passage?

   b. How does he contrast the works of the flesh and Spirit in verse 12?

   c. What does he say "not" to do in verse 13?

   d. What does he say "to do" in verse 14?

e. Since he doesn't give the particulars of our walk in verse 14, provide them here (that is, what does it mean to "put on the Lord Jesus Christ" in light of the preceding verse?):

4. What does the psalmist ask for in Psalm 143:10?

   a. What does he affirm about the Spirit? What does that mean?

   b. What three things does the psalmist want to be shown in Psalm 25:4–5?

   c. Why does he want these three things?

e. What is he willing to do until he receives the direction he seeks?

DID YOU KNOW?

It is possible to manifest one (or more) of the deeds of the flesh and still inherit the kingdom of God. But what of Paul's warning in Galatians 5:21—that no one practicing those deeds will inherit the kingdom? The key is in the grammar. When Paul says "those who practice such things" he uses a Greek form which implies ongoing, active, willful participation. Therefore, it would be impossible for one whose active, willing lifestyle is walking in the flesh to inherit God's kingdom. The kingdom is for those in whom the Spirit dwells, and who the Spirit has freed from slavery to the flesh. When that person's fleshly nature manifests itself, it is the exception, not the rule—an exception which God willingly forgives (1 John 1:9).

SUFFERING AND GLORY

Romans 8:17–18

In this lesson we learn the role of suffering in the spiritual life.

OUTLINE

Some Christians think having to attend church on Sunday night as well as Sunday morning is suffering for the Gospel. But suffering is a deeper subject than that. Understanding the biblical reasons for suffering can lead to spiritual consistency and maturity.

I. **The Relationship of Suffering to the Christian Life**

II. **The Reality of Suffering in the Christian Life**

III. **The Reasons for Suffering in the Christian Life**
   A. Suffering Proves the Reality of Our Faith
   B. Suffering Promotes Our Dependence Upon God
   C. Suffering Purifies Our Relationship With God
   D. Suffering Produces Endurance in Our Lives
   E. Suffering Prunes Us for Greater Effectiveness
   F. Suffering Provokes Courage in Other Believers
   G. Suffering Provides Opportunity for Witness
   H. Suffering Prepares Us to Reign With Christ

IV. **The Response to Suffering in the Christian Life**
   A. Preparation
   B. Memorization
   C. Dedication

J I. Packer offers a concise definition of suffering: "Getting what you do not want while wanting what you do not get."[1] There are many terms used in Scripture to talk about suffering—affliction, anguish, distress, grief, misery, pain, tribulation, chastisement, and others. Various metaphors also depict suffering, including refining fire (Isaiah 48:10; 1 Peter 1:6–7), overflowing waters (Isaiah 43:2), and birth pangs (John 16:20–22; Romans 8:18–22). All of these suggest what it feels like to suffer.

C. S. Lewis explained suffering like this:

Now God, who has made us, knows what we are and that our happiness lies in Him. Yet we will not seek it in Him as long as He leaves us any other resort where it can even plausibly be looked for. While what we call 'our own life' remains agreeable, we will not surrender it to Him. What then can God do in our interest but make 'our own life' less agreeable to us, and take away the plausible sources of false happiness.[2]

How does suffering fit within the broad context of the spiritual life?

THE RELATIONSHIP OF SUFFERING TO THE CHRISTIAN LIFE

Paul teaches that our ultimate reigning with Christ will be preceded by our suffering with Him. John Stott reminds us that suffering and glory belong together:

The sufferings and the glory belong together indissolubly. They did in the experience of Christ; they do in the experience of his people also. It is only after we 'have suffered a little while' that we will enter God's 'eternal glory in Christ,' to which he has called us. So the sufferings and the glory are married; they cannot be divorced. They are welded; they cannot be broken apart.[3]

THE REALITY OF SUFFERING IN THE CHRISTIAN LIFE

Leon Morris reminds us that suffering is our lot as Christians on this earth:

There is suffering that is the direct result of our sinning and there is suffering that we endure for Christ's sake, suffering that arises directly from our Christian profession in a world that rejects Christ. But beyond that, there is suffering that arises simply because we are in this imperfect world. Paul is realistic; there is no reason to think that Christians will be free from troubles in the present life. It is important, therefore, that they learn how to bear them.[4]

Many verses in the New Testament confirm Morris's words (John 15:18–20; 2 Corinthians 1:5; Philippians 1:29; 3:10; 2 Timothy 3:12; 1 Peter 4:12–13; 5:10).

John Piper's comments on this passage are worth meditating upon:

So we must not water down the call to suffer. We must not domesticate all the New Testament teaching on affliction and persecution just because our lives are so smooth. It may be that we have not chosen to live in all the radical ways of love that God wants us to. It may be that our time of suffering is just around the corner. But it will not do to take our own comfortable lives and make them the measure of what we allow the Bible to mean. Jesus came into the world to give his life as a ransom for many (Mark 10:45). There was a divine necessity upon him to suffer: 'The Son of Man must suffer many things' (Mark 8:31; cf. Luke 17:25). Because this was his vocation, suffering also becomes the vocation of those who follow him. It is implied in the words, 'As the Father has sent me, even so send I you' (John 20:21). And Jesus made it explicit when he said, 'Remember the word that I said to you, A servant is not greater than his master. If they persecuted me, they will persecute you' (John 15:20). 'If they have called the master of the house Beelzebub, how much more will they malign those of his household' (Matthew 10:25).[5]

THE REASONS FOR SUFFERING IN THE CHRISTIAN LIFE

The Bible reveals many reasons why suffering is part of the Christian walk.

Suffering Proves the Reality of Our Faith

Both Peter (1 Peter 1:7) and the writer to the Hebrews (Hebrews 12:5–11) connect suffering to the reality of one's faith. Suffering validates our confession.

Jonathan Chao, president of Christ's College, Taipei, and director for the Chinese Church Research Center in Hong Kong, has studied suffering in the context of the suffering of the church in China. He says, "One can almost say that suffering for Christ is a mark of discipleship."[6] Martyn Lloyd-Jones, who explores this line of thought extensively in his study of Romans 8:17, says, "If you are suffering as a Christian, and because you are a Christian, it is one of the surest proofs you can ever have of the fact that you are a child of God."[7]

Suffering Promotes Our Dependence Upon God

Scripture clearly suggests that we learn to trust God more when we suffer than when we don't (2 Corinthians 1:8–9; 12:9). Piper offers this word:

> God knocked the props of life out from under Paul's heart so that he would have no choice but to fall on God and get his hope from the promise of the Resurrection. This is the . . . purpose of . . . suffering: to wean us from the world and set our hope fully in God alone. Since the freedom to love flows from this kind of radical hope (Colossians 1:4–5), suffering is a primary means of building compassion into the lives of God's servants.[8]

Suffering Purifies Our Relationship With God

When we suffer, we are quickly able to focus on those things which are the priorities, which have the greatest value in life (Psalm 119:67, 71; Philippians 3:8, 10).

When the great French painter, Pierre Auguste Renoir, was afflicted with arthritis, his hands became twisted and deformed. Even holding a paint brush brought excruciating pain. When the artist Matisse watched him endure such pain he asked him why he was willing to endure such torture. Renoir replied, "The pain passes but the beauty remains."[9] When we endure suffering the beauty of the soul outlasts the agony we experience.

Suffering Produces Endurance in Our Lives

In an article that appeared in *Discipleship Journal,* Renee Rohrer explains why suffering is so beneficial to modern Christians:

> Patience is the supreme taunt to the West. It taunts us because we have grown up with the habit of immediacy. We have watched the deepest of human conflicts resolved in thirty minutes on a television screen. And we have come to expect of modern medicine a quick cure for every attack of disease.

To the West, endurance is synonymous with frustration. Small endurances bring on a stamping of the foot and a rearing of impatience. We honk the horn if the car ahead doesn't pull away when the light turns green. We mutter when waitresses take too long.

Is it any wonder then that we are undone—shattered—when we are held in the vice of a prolonged, difficult experience? We flail about helplessly. Thoughts of coping are overwhelming and bewildering. We don't want stamina—we want out.

Yet God in his tender mercy knows our frame. In spite of the indulgences of our culture, he moves ahead with us when we encounter suffering. Through it he begins to change the way we cope. He takes our impatience in hand. He ushers us into other realities. Things begin to happen to us, even apart from our cooperation . . . . God often moves the tape ten feet farther just when we think we're finishing the last lap of a race. Yet something happens in us when we've spent all we have and must still go on. When the work of the flesh is exhausted, perfection comes . . . . God is after more than our release.[10]

Suffering Prunes Us for Greater Effectiveness

For the grapevine, suffering is a way of life, the path to greater fruitfulness. The only way the vine produces a greater harvest is if the old branches are pruned away. So, God does His pruning work in our lives to bring forth even greater spiritual harvests (John 15:2).

Suffering Provokes Courage in Other Believers

The courage and sufferings of a young American missionary named David Brainerd (1718–1747) led hundreds of people to become missionaries. One such was Henry Martyn who recorded the impact of Brainerd's *Journal* in his own journal as he ministered in India: May 8, 1806: "Blessed be the memory of that holy man! I feel happy that I shall have his book with me in India, and thus enjoy, in a manner, the benefit of his company and example." May 12, 1806: "My soul was revived today through God's never-ceasing compassion, so that I found the refreshing presence of God in secret duties; especially was I most abundantly encouraged by reading Brainerd's account of the difficulties attending a mission to the heathen. Oh, blessed be the memory of that beloved saint!"[11]

In our own time it is hard to overstate the impact of the martyrdom of five young Wycliffe Bible Translators missionaries in Ecuador in 1956. Even more recently (1981), the execution of another Wycliffe missionary, Chet Bitterman, by a guerilla army group in Colombia had a mobilizing effect on college and university students. "In the year following Chet's death applications for overseas service with Wycliffe Bible Translators doubled. This trend was continued."[12]

Suffering Provides Opportunity for Witness

Suffering for the sake of the gospel has often been used to bring nonbelievers to Christ. Michael Card tells a story of a man named Joseph who was won to Christ from a Muslim background. He was so excited about his new relationship with God that he began pro-claiming Christ in his village. He was severely beaten and left for dead. He returned a few days later thinking he had confused the gospel message somehow, and began to preach again. For a second time he was beaten and left for dead outside the village. Upon recovering days later, he again entered the village but was attacked before he could even speak. When he regained consciousness after the third beating he discovered he was in his own bed being tended to by the women of the village. So convicted was the village by his courage and conviction and willingness to suffer that the entire village turned to Christ![13]

Suffering Prepares Us to Reign With Christ

John Piper writes,

Following Jesus means that wherever obedience requires it, we will accept betrayal and rejection and beating and mockery and crucifixion and death. Jesus gives us the assurance that if we will follow Him to Golgotha during all the Good Fridays of this life, we will also rise with Him on the last Easter day of the Resurrection. 'Whoever loses his life for my sake and the gospel's will save it.' (Mark 8:35). 'He who hates his life in this world will keep it for eternal life' (John 12:25).[14]

An aging Christian once objected to John G. Paton's plan to go as a missionary to the South Sea Islands with the words, 'You'll be eaten by Cannibals!' Paton responded: 'Mr. Dickson, you are advanced in years now, and your own prospect is soon to be laid in the grave, there to be eaten by worms; I confess to you, that if I can live and die serving and honoring the Lord Jesus, it will make no difference to me whether I am eaten by Cannibals or worms; and in the Great Day my resurrection body will arise fair as yours in the likeness of our risen Redeemer.'[15]

THE RESPONSE TO SUFFERING IN THE CHRISTIAN LIFE

Three aspects of the spiritual life are necessary to equip one to endure suffering and allow it to accomplish its intended purpose.

Preparation

Like the apostle Paul in his day (Acts 14:21–22; 1 Thessalonians 3:2–4), Richard Wurmbrand in our day knew the value of preparing to suffer. Wurmbrand was imprisoned and tortured for his faith for 14 years in his native Romania. He has written,

> I remember my last confirmation class before I left Romania. I took a group of ten to fifteen boys and girls on a Sunday morning, not to a church, but to the zoo. Before the cage of lions I told them, 'Your forefathers in faith were thrown before such wild beasts for their faith. Know that you also will have to suffer. You will not be thrown before lions, but you will have to do with men who would be much worse than lions. Decide here and now if you wish to pledge allegiance to Christ.' They had tears in their eyes when they said, Yes.

> We have to make the preparation now, before we are imprisoned. In prison you lose everything. You are undressed and given a prisoner's suit. No more nice furniture, nice carpets, or nice curtains. You do not have a wife any more and you do not have your children. You do not have your library and you never see a flower. Nothing of what makes life pleasant remains. Nobody resists who has not renounced the pleasures of life beforehand.[16]

Memorization

During times of suffering we gain great strength from verses of Scripture we have committed to memory, verses such as:

> "When you pass through the waters, I will be with you; And through the rivers, they shall not overflow you. When you walk through the fire, you shall not be burned, Nor shall the flame scorch you." (Isaiah 43:2)

> ". . . but rejoice to the extent that you partake of Christ's sufferings, that when His glory is revealed, you may also be glad with exceeding joy." (1 Peter 4:13)

"But may the God of all grace, who called us to His eternal glory by Christ Jesus, after you have suffered a while, perfect, establish, strengthen, and settle you. To Him be the glory and the dominion forever and ever. Amen." (1 Peter 5:10–11)

"Though I walk in the midst of trouble, You will revive me." (Psalm 138:7)

"And He said to me, 'My grace is sufficient for you, for My strength is made perfect in weakness.' Therefore most gladly I will rather boast in my infirmities, that the power of Christ may rest upon me." (2 Corinthians 12:9)

Dedication

These closing words are from the great British preacher Charles Haddon Spurgeon. They were written for preachers but they apply to us all:

"Serve God with all your might while the candle is burning, and then when it goes out for a season, you will have less to regret.

"Be content to be nothing, for that is what you are. When your own emptiness is painfully forced upon your consciousness, chide yourself that you ever dreamed of being full, except in the Lord.

"Continue with double earnestness to serve your Lord when no visible result is before you. Any simpleton can follow the narrow path in the light: Faith's rare wisdom enables us to march on in the dark with infallible accuracy, since she places her hand in that of her Great Guide."[17]

Notes:

1. J. I. Packer, *Rediscovering Holiness* (Ann Arbor: Servant Publications, 1992), 249.

2. C. S. Lewis, *The Problem of Pain* (New York: MacMillan, 1962), 93.

3. John Stott, *Romans: God's Good News For The World* (Downer's Grove: InterVarsity Press, 1994), 237.

4. Leon Morris, *The Epistle To The Romans* (Grand Rapids: InterVarsity Press, 1994), 319.

5. John Piper, *Let The Nations Be Glad - The Supremacy Of God In Missions* (Grand Rapids: Baker Books, 1993), 74–75.

6. Jonathan Chao, "Witness In Suffering," a paper prepared for the Second Asian Leadership Conference on Evangelism, Singapore, October 20–27, 1987, 7.

7. D. Martyn Lloyd-Jones, *Romans: An Exposition of Chapter 8:5–17* (Grand Rapids: Zondervan, 1974), 433.

8. John Piper, 87–88.

9. Quoted by Harold Sala in *Answers To Suffering* (Manilla: OMF Publishers, 1986), n.p.

10. *Discipleship Journal,* September 1, 1983, 27, 29.

11. *Journal and Letters of Henry Martyn* (New York: Protestant Episcopal Society For The Promotion of Evangelical Knowledge, 1851), 240, 326–328.

12. Steve Estes, *Called to Die* (Grand Rapids: Zondervan Corporation, 1986), 252.

13. Michael Card, "Wounded in the House of Friends," Virtue, March/April 1991, 28–29, 69.

14. John Piper, 75.

15. James Paton, ed., *John G. Paton: Missionary to the New Hebrides, An Autobiography* (London: The Banner of Truth Trust, 1965, originally 1891), 56.

16. Richard Wurmbrand, "Preparing the Underground Church," In: Epiphany Journal, 5/4 Summer, 1985, 46–48.

17. Charles Haddon Spurgeon, "The Minister's Fainting Fits," in *Lectures To My Students* (Grand Rapids: Zondervan, 1972), 164–165.

APPLICATION

The Scriptures are filled with truths about suffering as a believer. Record your insights about suffering from this sampling of verses.

1. What is in store for the Christian even though he suffers? (1 Peter 5:10)

2. How likely is it that committed Christians will suffer? (2 Timothy 3:12)

3. How would you define "the fellowship of His sufferings?" (Philippians 3:10)

4. How does Peter suggest we view trials and suffering? (1 Peter 4:12–13)

5. When we suffer for our faith, for whose sake are we suffering? (Philippians 1:29)

6. How does the teacher-disciple relationship apply to suffering? (John 15:18–20)

7. How do trials relate to the genuineness of faith? (1 Peter 1:6–7)

8. Describe why God sometimes deliberately causes His children to suffer. (Hebrews 12:5–11)

9. In the final analysis, what does the believer trust in while suffering? (2 Corinthians 1:8–9)

10. When you are made weak through suffering, what is made strong? (2 Corinthians 12:9)

11. How can suffering have a positive result? (Psalm 119:67, 71)

12. What does the testing of your faith produce? (James 1:3–4)

13. What must happen in order for you to bear more fruit for God? (John 15:2)

14. When other Christians see you suffering faithfully, what are they encouraged to do? (Philippians 1:14)

15. What must happen before new life can be revealed? (John 12:24; 2 Corinthians 4:10)

16. Why might God put you in a place of suffering? (Philippians 1:12–13)

17. For those willing to suffer with Christ, what will they ultimately enjoy? (Romans 8:17)

18. How is God's righteous judgment manifested at times?
    (2 Thessalonians 1:4–5)

19. Explain the meaning of 2 Timothy 2:12 as it relates
    to suffering:

20. Explain Paul's calm perspective concerning suffering.
    (1 Thessalonians 3:2–4)

21. With what is the road to the kingdom of God paved?
    (Acts 14:21–22)

22. To what was Paul called and appointed in his ministry
    as an apostle? (Acts 9:15–16)

DID YOU KNOW?

In its first few centuries, the church endured great persecution throughout the Roman Empire. A leader of the church in North Africa by the name of Tertullian responded with a statement to Rome that has fueled the church's courage ever since: "However often we are mown down by you, we increase in numbers; it is Christian blood that is the seed." Tertullian's statement has been shortened through the centuries to become the battle cry of all who suffer persecution for Jesus' sake: "The blood of the martyrs is the seed of the church!" In our comfortable day of creative church growth strategies, the shedding of blood is rarely mentioned as a method. But throughout history, the church has never failed to grow when it has suffered.

GROANING AND GLORY

Romans 8:17–27

*In this lesson we discover the source of groanings
in our world.*

OUTLINE

Many people are familiar with only one kind of groaning—their own
at the end of a hard day at work. But groaning is actually much
deeper, and more spiritual, than that. To understand the Bible's
three kinds of groans is to understand the present—and the future.

I. **The Groaning of the Creation**
   A. What This Groaning Is Not
   B. What This Groaning Is

II. **The Groaning of the Christians**
   A. Three Negative Reasons for Our Groaning
   B. Three Positive Reasons for Our Groaning

III. **The Groaning of the Comforter**
   A. What This Groaning Is Not
   B. What This Groaning Is

IV. **From Groaning to Glory**
   A. The Priority of Hope
   B. The Perspective of Eternity
   C. The Presence of the Holy Spirit

Our focus for this lesson actually begins in verse 17. We devoted the entire last lesson to exploring the theme of suffering which Paul discusses in verses 17 and 18. In those two verses Paul introduced what we will cover in this lesson: groanings and glory. He stated that the groanings (sufferings) we endure in this life are not worthy to be compared to the glory which will be revealed in us one day.

This truth was something Paul considered carefully, or meditated upon (verse 18). It could be taken as a judgment, or decision on his part which represented a conviction in his life: Though we suffer in this life, our future glory is what guides us through our groanings. There are three specific kinds of groanings Paul will mention in verses 19–27.

THE GROANING OF THE CREATION (8:19–22)

The word for "groaning," which Paul uses three times in Romans, chapter 8, is a derivative of *stenazo* which means "to sigh or groan because of an undesired circumstance." In order to arrive at what this groaning is about, we need to eliminate what it is not about.

What This Groaning Is Not

The groaning does not refer to Satan and his fallen angels or even to created angels who were not subjected to the "bondage of corruption." Neither of these classes of created beings could be said to long for the manifestation of the sons of God nor will they share in the "glorious liberty of the children of God." Nor is it the groaning of unbelievers—the "earnest expectation" does not apply to them. Finally, it is not the groaning of believers as they are mentioned separately in verses 19, 21, and 23.

What This Groaning Is

This is a reference to the non-rational animate and inanimate creation. It includes the animals, the trees, mountains, rivers, plains, and heavenly bodies. Paul pictures this part of creation as an audience eagerly waiting for the sons of God to come into their true glory. The sense of the Greek words Paul uses is captured by the J. B. Phillips translation: "The whole creation is on tiptoe to see the wonderful sight of the sons of God coming into their own."

This groaning of creation began with the fall of Adam and Eve into sin.

When Adam fell, the entire 'creation' suffered the results of sin (Gen. 3:17–18). Primitive domesticity among the animals was lost, and decadence became apparent in every aspect of the universe. All of this creation groans and labors awaiting the day when, it too, shall be delivered from the bondage of its corruption into the liberty of the children of God. Ultimately, the efficacy of Christ's redemptive work at Golgotha extends even to the sin-cursed cosmos itself. This event transpires during the kingdom age or Millennium (Revelation 20:1–10). Jesus himself spoke of the restitution of all things (Matthew 19:28).[1]

Paul describes the present condition of creation as subjected to futility. The word translated "frustration" is the Greek word *mataiotes* and it means the inability to fulfill the purpose for which something was created. It can also mean emptiness, futility, or even absurdity. The harder man tries the bigger his problems become:

Our knowledge leaps exponentially and our problems no less so. Books increase and ignorance prevails, harvests increase and hunger spreads, production grows and poverty deepens. Mechanization makes our lives easier but threatens our worth as persons, and the time it saves us gives us time to consider the meaninglessness of life around us. . . . Symbolic of our being subjected to frustration is our nuclear weaponry which, with each advance in technology, makes our lives and world less secure. Human solutions, which once promised to perfect our world, now seem woefully inadequate to even preserve our world.[2]

Many ideas have been set forth as to the meaning of verse 21. How will creation be liberated from its bondage to decay and brought into the glorious freedom of the children of God? James Montgomery Boice has a good analogy in his commentary on Romans:

Perhaps the closest we can come (and still be fairly sure we are on the right track) is by an analogy to 'the redemption of our bodies,' which is brought into the picture in verse 24. The redemption of our bodies means the resurrection of our bodies. So perhaps this is what creation will experience, a resurrection. In our resurrections we will have a continuity of our bodies (our earthly bodies will be raised), but our bodies will be different, heavenly, glorified. Creation will probably experience something like that, too.[3]

We are now living in the travail of labor. Kent Hughes pictures the present, and future, beautifully:

> Many of us have pictures of our wives after they have delivered a child, and typically the baby is in their arms and the mother is radiant. None of us have a picture of our wives in labor. We do not reach into our wallets saying, 'Let me show you a picture of Margaret groaning in labor. Isn't the agony terrific?' Creation will one day be delivered and the difference between then and now is the difference between agony and ecstasy![4]

THE GROANING OF THE CHRISTIANS (8:23)

Not only does the whole of creation groan, but Christians groan as well—"earnestly desiring to be clothed with our habitation which is from heaven" (2 Corinthians 5:2). There are three negative and three positive reasons why Christians groan at the present time.

Three Negative Reasons for Our Groaning

1. We groan because of the presence of sin in the world.

   Ray Stedman points out, "We groan because of the ravages that sin makes in our lives and in the lives of those we love. Also we groan because we see possibilities that are not being captured and employed. And then we groan because we see gifted people who are wasting their lives, and we would love to see something else happening. It is recorded that, as He drew near the tomb of Lazarus, Jesus groaned in His spirit because He was so burdened by the ravages that sin had made in a believing family. He groaned, even though He knew he would soon raise Lazarus from the dead. So we groan in our spirits—we groan in disappointment, in bereavement, in sorrow. We groan physically in our pain and our limitation. Life consists of a great deal of groaning."[5]

2. We groan because of the power of sin in our bodies.

   Who of us in our desire to be holy have not found ourselves groaning over the intrusion of sin into our lives? In Romans seven Paul is describing this very agony as he groaned these words: "O wretched man that I am! Who will deliver me from this body of death?" (Romans 7:24) Paul viewed the continuing influence of sin in his body to be like dragging a corpse around all day long—groan!

3. We groan because of the practice of sin by those around us.

   This is not an attempt to blame others for our troubles; rather it is a statement of reality. We often suffer innocently when others sin whether at a personal or a corporate level. The African proverb, "When elephants fight, the grass gets trampled," says it well.

Three Positive Reasons for Our Groaning

1. We groan because we have been given the Holy Spirit to guarantee our glory.

   "The firstfruits of the Spirit" was a phrase which Paul's Jewish readers would have understood. In the Old Testament, Jews were required to bring the firstfruits of their harvest and present them before the Lord as a symbol that the whole harvest belonged to Him (Leviticus 23:10–11). Here, Paul uses the image in reverse, saying that the giving of the Holy Spirit to believers is the first sign or guarantee of our complete salvation which is to come.

   John Stott writes: "So the Holy Spirit, who is the Spirit of sonship and makes us the children of God (verse 15), and then witnesses with our spirit that we are God's children (verse 16), is also himself the pledge of our complete adoption to be the sons of God, when our bodies are redeemed."[6]

2. We groan because we look forward to our adoption being final.

   While we are legally adopted by God at the moment of our conversion, the experience of our adoption is not made complete until we are in His presence in glory. Paul was using the Roman concept of adoption which was much like the Jewish Bar Mitzvah. A passage in the famous novel *The Robe* pictures Roman adoption. Marcellus is describing his adoption to a friend named Paulus:

   When a Roman of our sort comes of age, Paulus, there is an impressive ceremony by which we are inducted into manhood . . . . Well do I remember—the thrill of it abides with me still—how all of our relatives and friends assembled that day, in the stately Forum Julium. My father made an address, welcoming me into Roman citizenship. It was as if I had never lived until that hour. I was so deeply stirred, Paulus, that my eyes swam with tears. And then good old

Cornelius Capito made a speech, a very serious one, about Rome's right to my loyalty, my courage, my strength. I knew that tough old Capito had a right to talk of such matters, and I was proud that he was there! They beckoned to me, and I stepped forward. Capito and my father put the white Toga on me—and life had begun![7]

3. We groan because we anticipate the redemption of the body.

Our bodies are the center of our physical weaknesses and the home of our sinful natures. No wonder we groan in them! We groan knowing that someday these bodies are going to be redeemed and transformed into glorious bodies like the resurrection body of the Lord Jesus Christ (Philippians 3:20–21).

THE GROANING OF THE COMFORTER (8:26–27)

Finally, we see that the Holy Spirit Himself groans—but He does so in our behalf. There are times when we are unable to pray, when we are under such pressure and in such pain that we cannot verbalize our desires. Paul says that when those times come the Holy Spirit Himself intercedes for us with groans that words cannot express.

What This Groaning Is Not

This is not, as some have taught, a proof text for speaking in tongues.

Some have interpreted this verse as arguing for 'prayer tongues.' However, close examination reveals that the believer is not speaking at all. The Holy Spirit is making the intercession. Moreover, the precise words in Greek are *stenagmois alaletois*, 'groanings which cannot be uttered.' Literally, the words might be rendered 'unspoken sighings.' In other words, the communication is nonverbal, involving no speaking of any kind.[8]

What This Groaning Is

The Believer's Study Bible accurately pictures the purpose of the Holy Spirit's groaning:

Among the benefits of adoption into God's family is the special supernatural care bestowed by the Holy Spirit upon the child of God. The Holy Spirit is present within the Christian to assist him in those moments of moral, physical, or emotional weakness. Frequently a disciple confronts difficulties so insurmountable that he cannot even approach prayer skillfully. He knows that he must approach God, but he has already said all that he knows to say to God. In those instances, the promise is that the Holy Spirit 'makes intercession for us with groanings which cannot be uttered.'[9]

Here is the point of Paul's detailed description of our "groanings." Recall how he started this section: "For I consider that the sufferings of this present time are not worthy to be compared with the glory which shall be revealed in us" (Romans 8:18). Paul is asking us to see our present sufferings and groanings in light of eternal joy and glory. This is pictured even more graphically in 2 Corinthians: "For our light affliction, which is but for a moment, is working for us a far more exceeding and eternal weight of glory, while we do not look at the things which are seen, but at the things which are not seen. For the things which are seen are temporary, but the things which are not seen are eternal" (2 Corinthians 4:17–18).

Note the contrasts that are in focus here:

outward man	inward man
perishing	being renewed day by day
light	weight
for a moment	eternal
affliction	glory
seen	unseen
temporary	eternal

For the believer to survive amidst the many challenges in this world, he must keep an eternal perspective. It is his only source of true meaning and peace in a fallen world.

FROM GROANING TO GLORY

Though ultimate glory is a future reality for the believer, we can experience a foretaste of that glory in this life by practicing three disciplines in the spiritual life.

The Priority of Hope

Consider the words of Martyn Lloyd-Jones:

True Christianity . . . is not primarily concerned even with the deliverance from hell, and punishment, and all the things that trouble us and weary us. This really belongs to the past. True

Christianity 'sets its affection on things which are above, not on the things which are on the earth.' It is that which says, 'We look not at the things which are seen, but at the things which are not seen; for the things which are seen are temporal, but the things which are not seen are eternal.' [10]

The Perspective of Eternity

One of the blessings of our groanings is that we are forced to focus on eternity. James Boice explains how an eternal focus affects our present life:

> You will not be surprised when things go wrong in this life. This world is not a good place. We live in a fallen environment. Your plans will misfire, you will often fail, others will destroy what you have spent long years and much toil to accomplish. This will be true even if you are a Christian and are trying to follow Jesus. But our successes are not what life is all about. What matters is our love for God and our faithfulness. [11]

The Presence of the Holy Spirit

What is really involved in the Holy Spirit's groaning in our behalf?

> Obviously it does not mean that the Holy Spirit is unable to articulate his concerns. Yet if the idea of bearing a heavy burden is in view, it may be that this is what is governing the apostle's thought. A groan is appropriate to burden bearing.

> Suppose you are helping someone carry a heavy load. What is more expressive: a groan as you stagger along beneath it or a great deal of articulate chatter? . . . A real burden-bearer groans with you. I suggest that this is the image Paul is using. [12]

Knowing that the Holy Spirit is helping us to bear the burdens of this life through prayer can help us keep our fixed on the glory ahead.

Notes:

1. *The Believer's Study Bible,* W. A. Criswell, Ed. (Nashville: Thomas Nelson, 1991), 1610.

2. Notes On Romans - Lesson 16 - *Community Bible Study* (Maclean: VA, 1983–84), 3.

3. James Montgomery Boice, *Romans - Volume Two - The Reign of Grace* - Romans 5–8 (Grand Rapids: Baker Book House, 1992), 874.

4. Kent Hughes, *Romans- Righteousness From Heaven* (Wheaton: Crossway Books, 1991), 160.

5. Ray C. Stedman, *From Guilt To Glory,* Volume 1 (Waco: Word, 1981), 241.

6. John R. W. Scott, *Men made New: An Exposition of Romans 5–8* (Grand Rapids: Baker Book House, 1984), 97.

7. Lloyd C. Douglas, *The Robe* (Boston: Houghton Mifflin, 1945), 66.

8. *The Believer's Study Bible,* 1611.

9. *The Believer's Study Bible,* 1611.

10. D. Martyn Lloyd-Jones, *Romans - Final Perseverance of the Saints* - Exposition of Chapter 8:17–39 (Grand Rapids: Zondervan Publishing Co., 1975), 104.

11. James Montgomery Boice, 875.

12. James Montgomery Boice, 890.

APPLICATION

1. Read Genesis 3:17–19.

   a. What pronouncement did God make concerning the ground of this earth (the creation)? (verse 17)

   b. For what reason was the earth cursed? (verse 17)

   c. What impact was God's curse to have upon Adam (all mankind)? (verses 17b–19a)

   d. Given the condition of life upon earth as a result of the curse, what do you think life might have been like on earth had there been no curse?

   e. What signs of the curse do you see around you?

   f. Even though you may not make your living from the soil, what evidences of the curse on creation do you experience in your personal life?

2. Read Isaiah 11:6–9.

   a. List all the pairs of "natural enemies" that are pictured as being at peace with one another:

   b. What seems to be the cause of this reversal of the curse upon creation? (verse 9b)

   c. How are hurting and destroying an evidence of the groaning which all creation labors under at present? (verse 9a)

   d. Who appears responsible for bringing about this universal reign of peace? (Isaiah 11:1–5, 10)

   e. Who is the "Rod from the stem of Jesse"? (verse 1)

3. Read Isaiah 35:1; 55:12; 65:17.

   a. What signs do you see in 35:1 and 55:12 that creation longs to experience something more glorious than it does at present?

   b. What is God going to do to restore creation to its former glory? (65:17)

   c. What will happen to the first heaven and earth? (Revelation 21:1)

   d. How does Peter describe the day when this re-creation will take place? (2 Peter 3:10–11a)

4. Read Philippians 3:20–21; 1 Corinthians 15:50–58.

   a. How do we know that our true home is not this earth?
      (Philippians 3:20)

   b. What will happen to our "lowly body" in which we groan at
      present? (verse 21a)

   c. How is Christ able to transform us from groaning to glory?
      (verse 21b)

   d. Why do we need to be changed from the condition in which
      we inhabit this earth? (1 Corinthians 15:50)

e. When will our transformation into glory take place? (verse 52)

f. The curse on creation brought death into the world. What will happen to death in the end? (verses 54–55)

g. What is the only source of victory, of release from the groaning of this life? (verse 57)

h. What impact should the truth of our future final redemption have on our lives now? (verse 58)

DID YOU KNOW?

One of the greatest evidences of the earth being created by the hand of a powerful and wise God is its ability to "heal" itself. Just as the human body has the ability to fight off infections and heal its own wounds, so the earth continues to renew itself even as it labors under the curse of creation. Efforts in recent decades to focus on cleaning up and preserving the environment have shown how resilient God's creation is. Polluted rivers become clean, dirty air becomes breathable, and forests renew themselves. It is as though a vibrant creation lurks beneath the surface, waiting to reveal the majesty and wisdom of its Creator. Until that day, we should honor the handiwork of God by doing what we can to preserve and protect all His creation.

A SOFT PILLOW FOR TIRED HEARTS

Romans 8:28

In this lesson we discover how to live with certainty in every circumstance.

OUTLINE

Lots of people believe everything happens for a reason, but only Christians can know for sure. Rather than trusting in fate, believers live by faith in a loving God who causes all of life's puzzle-pieces to fit together to form a beautiful, complete picture.

   I. **This Is a Definite Promise: "And We Know"**

  II. **This Is a Divine Promise: "God Works"**

 III. **This Is a Determined Promise: "For the Good of His People"**

  IV. **This Is a Definitive Promise: "All Things"**

   V. **This Is a Dynamic Promise: "Work Together"**

  VI. **This Is a Defined Promise: "Those Who Love God"**
   A. Those Who Love Him
   B. Those Who Are Called

 VII. **This Is a Demonstrable Promise**
   A. Job
   B. Jacob
   C. Joseph
   D. Jewish Nation
   E. Jeremiah
   F. Jesus

VIII. **The Believer's Response to Romans 8:28**
   A. It Fills the Believer With Trust
   B. It Fills the Believer With Thanksgiving
   C. It Fills the Believer With Tenacity

The last 12 verses of Romans chapter 8 may be unequaled anywhere else in the New Testament. John Stott's summary is excellent:

These tremendous truths the apostle declares three times over, although from three different perspectives. He begins with five unshakeable convictions (28) about God working all things together for the good of his people. He continues with five undeniable affirmations (29–30) regarding the successive states of God's saving purpose from eternity to eternity. And he concludes with five unanswerable questions (31–39), in which he challenges anybody to contradict the convictions and affirmations which he has just expressed.[1]

The first of these 12 dynamic verses is the focus of our study in this lesson. Next to John 3:16, it may be the most well-known and oft-quoted verses in the Bible. Look at what a number of Bible commentators have said about Romans 8:28:

John Stott: "Romans 8:28 is surely one of the best-known texts in the Bible. On it believers of every age and place have stayed their minds."[2]

R. A. Torrey: "Romans 8:28 is a soft pillow for a tired heart."[3]

John MacArthur: "For Christians, this verse contains perhaps the most glorious promise in Scripture. It is breathtaking in its magnitude, encompassing absolutely everything that pertains to a believer's life."[4]

John Phillips: "This is a great verse, often quoted in times of distress . . . . Like the cogs in an intricate piece of machinery, all things work together for good to the called of God for the simple reason that God's purposes cannot be thwarted."[5]

THIS IS A DEFINITE PROMISE: "AND WE KNOW"

"We know" is used five times in the book of Romans and the word "know" is used 13 times. It refers to that which is the common knowledge of believers. Paul says we can know beyond all doubt that every aspect of our lives is in God's hands and will be divinely used by the Lord not only to manifest His own glory but to work out our own ultimate blessing.

Barnhouse has a great word here:

We know . . . that is the tremendous fact of this verse. It would be wonderful if all things worked together for our good without our knowing it, and we would find out about it later. But it is possible here and now for us to know that all things work together for our good. To lay hold of that fact is to calm the turbulence of life and to bring quiet and confidence into the whole of life. Nothing can touch me unless it passes through the will of God. God has a plan for my life. God is working according to a fixed, eternal purpose.[6]

Earlier in this same context, Paul said we know about the groaning of creation (verse 22) and here he says we know of God's providential care. Yet in verse 26 he says we sometimes don't know how to pray as we ought. I don't think this juxtaposition is accidental; it illustrates a tension in the Christian life. We know that God is ultimately in control in this life, but sometimes we don't know how all the pieces fit together. One of the paradoxes of the Christian life is this: We are often the most certain about the ultimate when we are the most uncertain about the immediate.

THIS IS A DIVINE PROMISE: "GOD WORKS"

Paul is not saying that everything will always work out alright if we just wait. He is not speaking fatalistically, nor is he espousing a "positive mental attitude" as a solution when we don't understand. This promise does not operate through impersonal statements, but requires divine action in order for it to be fulfilled. The order of the words in this verse helps us to see what Paul is really saying: "We know that for those who love God, He is working."

In other words, "God is ceaselessly, energetically, and purposefully active on their behalf." It is God Himself who is bringing this good about in behalf of those who love Him.

THIS IS A DETERMINED PROMISE: "FOR THE GOOD OF HIS PEOPLE"

God is at work for the good of His people. Since God is good, the work that He is doing for His people is good. The ultimate good toward which He is working is the final salvation and glorification of His children. This is evident from verses 29 and 30.

Paul tells us here that God causes all things to work together for good. The "all things" are like the pieces of a giant jigsaw puzzle. The way they work together for the good is that they work according to God's purpose. His purpose is like the picture on the lid of the puzzle box. He knows what the completed puzzle picture looks like even when we do not, and He is putting all the pieces in place to cause the picture to be completed perfectly and according to His purpose.

THIS IS A DEFINITIVE PROMISE: "ALL THINGS"

The "all things" of this verse is totally comprehensive. It has no limits. Taken in its context, the promise allows for no restrictions or conditions. "All things" includes the "sufferings" of verse 17 and the "groanings" of verse 23. In other words, all that is negative in this life is seen to have a positive purpose in the execution of God's eternal plan. Nothing is beyond the overruling, overriding scope of His providence.

Paul is not saying that evil things are good. "But what the text teaches . . . is that God uses these things to effect his own good ends for people. God brings good out of evil . . . ."[7] Nor is he saying that God always keep His children from experiencing hurtful things.

He is rather attesting that the Lord takes all that He allows to happen to His beloved children, even the worst things, and turns those things ultimately into blessings . . . . No matter what our situation, our suffering, our persecution, our sinful failure, our pain, our lack of faith—in those things, as well as in all other things, our heavenly Father will work to produce our ultimate victory and blessing.[8]

Paul is not expressing faith in the goodness of all things but in the goodness and sovereignty of God!

Barnhouse summarizes by saying,

There is no will or act of creatures, men, angels or demons that can do other than work for our good. No dog can bark against us, no man can speak or act against us, no sinister power of evil can be against us, but all must be for our good. There is no phenomenon of nature—fire, flood, storm, earthquake—that can work us ultimate ill. The law of gravity cannot trip us up or cause anything to fall upon us unless it has first been sifted through the will of God's purpose for our good. Every experience of our individual circumstances, whether temptations, or whatever concerns us, humbles us and forces us to rely on Him, who alone can satisfy. All things work together for our good; otherwise the Lord would not permit them.[9]

THIS IS A DYNAMIC PROMISE: "WORK TOGETHER"

"Together" translates the Greek word *sunergeo*. It is the word from which we get our word synergism. Synergism is the working together of various elements to produce an effect greater than, and often completely different from, the sum of each element acting separately. In the physical world, the right combination of otherwise harmful chemicals can produce substances that are extremely beneficial. For example, ordinary table salt is composed of two poisons, sodium and chlorine.

Once again it is important to point out that this is not saying that things will just work out. It is saying that God causes this synergism to happen. He is the One who stirs the mix!

THIS IS A DEFINED PROMISE: "THOSE WHO LOVE GOD"

This is the only limitation contained in this promise. Paul is not expressing a general, superficial optimism that everything tends toward everybody's good in the end. Rather, he uses two terms to describe those who are the recipients of this promise. He says that they are those who love God and those who are the called.

"Those who love God" looks at these people from the human perspective, and "those who are the called" looks at them from God's perspective.

Those Who Love Him

"Those who love God" is the fraternity pin of the believer. Loving God puts one in a distinct class of human beings, separate from all others. Those who, from the human point of view, have chosen to direct their love toward God are the ones who may be assured that all things work together for good. Why? Because as Paul says in 1 Corinthians 8:3, ". . . if anyone loves God, this one is known by Him."

Those Who Are Called

Being called by God is not a reference to those who have received an invitation and responded. This calling is much deeper than that. This calling is part of the process that Paul will explain in verses 29 and 30. From our standpoint we are believers because we love God. But from God's viewpoint, we are believers because we are called by Him unto salvation.

F. F. Bruce refers to the Westminster Shorter Catechism and defines this calling like this: "The 'called,' not in the general sense in which 'many are called, but few are chosen'; but in the sense of that 'effectual calling' which is the work of God's Spirit, whereby, convincing us of our sin and misery, enlightening our minds in the knowledge of Christ, and renewing our wills, He doth persuade and enable us to embrace Jesus Christ, freely offered to us in the gospel."[10]

THIS IS A DEMONSTRABLE PROMISE

All through Scripture we have examples of those who learned to trust God in the midst of their very difficult circumstances—and who ultimately saw the good that God accomplished.

Job

Job was a man who lost everything he had even though he was a righteous man who "feared God and shunned evil" (Job 1:1). His property, his livestock, his possessions, even his children were taken from him through a series of disasters. Finally, even his health was taken from him. But through it all Job believed that the Lord gives and the Lord takes away and blessed is His name (Job 1:21). Job believed he would come through the test as gold through the fire (Job 23:10). Through his circumstances he gained a knowledge of God that he had never had (Job 42:4–6) and was blessed far beyond his original condition (Job 42:12).

Jacob

Jacob reaped the harvest of his younger years. Joseph was gone; Reuben was disgraced; Judah was dishonored; Simeon and Levi had broken his heart; Dinah was defiled; Simeon was in prison; beloved Rachel was dead; famine threatened the family. Then came the demand from Egypt that young Benjamin must appear there before its awesome governor before any further supplies would be released. Jacob felt that everything was aligned against him (Genesis 42:36). Yet all these things were working together to keep his family, and God's promises, alive for future generations.

Joseph

Joseph, the son of Jacob, was sold into slavery by his brothers. When he earned favor in Egypt by interpreting Pharaoh's dream, he was made the number two man over all the country. When he was ultimately reunited with his brothers, he saw that God had sent him ahead to prepare a place for Jacob's family to survive the famine in Canaan. As he told his brothers when they realized with shame that Joseph had become their salvation, ". . . you meant evil against me; but God meant it for good, in order to bring it about as it is this day, to save many people alive" (Genesis 50:20).

Jewish Nation

After delivering the Israelites from Egyptian bondage, God continually provided for their well-being as they faced the harsh obstacles of the Sinai desert. As Moses proclaimed the Law to Israel, he reminded the people:

"[God] who led you through the great and terrible wilderness, in which were fiery serpents and scorpions, and a thirsty land where there was no water; who brought water for you out of the flinty rock; who fed you in the wilderness with manna, which your fathers did not know, that He might test you, to do you good in the end . . ." (Deuteronomy 8:15–16).

Jeremiah

At a time when the Jews were about to be carried away into Babylon after the terrible destruction of Jerusalem, God gave them a promise through Jeremiah about their future: "For I know the thoughts that I think toward you, says the Lord, thoughts of peace and not of evil, to give you a future and a hope" (Jeremiah 29:11). Regardless of what sort of calamity they were experiencing, it was not as a result of evil intentions by God, but of good.

Jesus

In the life of His own Son, God took the most absolute evil that Satan could devise and turned it into the greatest conceivable blessing He could offer to fallen mankind—eternal salvation from sin. Jesus was "delivered by the determined purpose and fore-knowledge of God . . . crucified, and put to death" (Acts 2:23). The only way Jesus could have submitted to the Father in the face of death was to know that God's absolute good purposes were ruling over all.

THE BELIEVER'S RESPONSE TO ROMANS 8:28

This great verse of Scripture can fill the believer with trust, thanksgiving, and tenacity when it is embraced and relied upon in every circumstance of life.

It Fills the Believer With Trust

"For I am God, and there is no other; I am God and there is none like Me, declaring the end from the beginning, and from ancient times things that are not yet done, saying, 'My counsel shall stand, And I will do all My pleasure . . . . Indeed, I have spoken it; I will also bring it to pass. I have purposed it, I will also do it'"(Isaiah 46:9–11).

It Fills the Believer With Thanksgiving

"Giving thanks always for all things to God the Father in the name of our Lord Jesus Christ" (Ephesians 5:20).

"In everything give thanks; for this is the will of God in Christ Jesus for you" (1 Thessalonians 5:18).

It Fills the Believer With Tenacity

"Therefore we do not lose heart. Even though our outward man is perishing, yet the inward man is being renewed day by day. For our light affliction, which is but for a moment, is working for us a far more exceeding and eternal weight of glory" (2 Corinthians 4:16–17).

Rather than trusting in fate or blind faith, the child of God has the privilege of thankfully trusting in a loving God while living life pro-actively every day, never fearing the future or what it might bring.

Notes:

1. John Stott, *Romans: God's Good News For the World* (Downers Grove: InterVarsity Press, 1994), 246.

2. John Stott, 246.

3. Attributed to R. A Torrey, source unknown.

4. John MacArthur, *The MacArthur New Testament Commentary* - Romans 1–8 (Chicago: Moody Press, 1991), 471.

5. John Phillips, *Exploring Romans* (Chicago: Moody Press, 1969), 134.

6. Donald Grey Barnhouse, *Romans, God's Heirs* - Romans 8:1–39 (Grand Rapids: Wm. B. Eerdman's Publishing Co., 1959), 153.

7. James Montgomery Boice, *Romans - Volume Two - The Reign Of Grace* - Romans 5–8 (Grand Rapids: Baker Book House, 1992), 906.

8. John MacArthur, 473.

9. Donald Grey Barnhouse, 158.

10. F. F. Bruce, *The Epistle Of Paul To The Romans*, Tyndale New Testament Commentaries (Grand Rapids: Eerdmans Publishing Co., 1963), 176.

1. Read Romans 8:30–32.

    a. What support do you find in each of these verses for the idea that God causes all things to work together for good for His children?

       • Verse 30:

       • Verse 31:

       • Verse 32:

2. Read 2 Corinthians 4:7–15.

    a. What did Paul mean by a treasure in earthen vessels? (verse 7; see verse 1)

    b. How easily broken are earthen vessels?

    c. Why did God deposit a treasure as great as the gospel in something so easily broken as a clay vessel (human being)? (verse 7)

d. How does Paul describe the hardship his "vessel" endured in the ministry of the gospel? (verses 8–9)

e. If his vessel was broken, what would shine forth even more? (verses 10–11)

e. How can death and life be at work in the same set of circumstances? (verse 12)

f. Even if Paul's vessel had been completely shattered, what good result would eventually come of it? (verses 13–14)

g. What ultimate good was being brought out of Paul's dire circumstances as he traveled about sharing the gospel? (verse 15)

3. Read 2 Corinthians 12:7–10.

a. What was the difficult circumstance Paul found himself in? (verse 7)

b. How did he try to remedy the situation? (verse 8)

c. What precedent does Paul set in trying to "fix" difficult circumstances? That is, is it more spiritual to passively accept difficulty than to try to correct it?

d. What answer did God give Paul about his circumstances? (verse 9a)

e. How did this answer turn out to be "good" for Paul? (verses 9b–10)

f. How would you feel about a difficulty being for your good if you knew the only good coming from it was that Christ was magnified through you?

g. What do we normally think of as "good" when we think of the promise in Romans 8:28? How would you feel if the "good" that came from your difficulties was entirely for the benefit of others, not yourself?

4. Read Acts 7:54–8:1.

   a. What was the difficult circumstance confronting Stephen?

   b. Who was their observing what happened to Stephen? (verse 58; 8:1a)

   c. What impact do you think this even might have had on Paul later in his life?

   d. What positive impact on church growth resulted from Stephen's death? (8:1b, 4)

DID YOU KNOW?

When Paul wrote Romans 8:28–39—and especially verse 28—he was stepping on some traditional religious toes in the Mediterranean world. In Greek mythology, there were three goddesses who determined human life and destiny. These goddesses, the Fates, set apart a share of good and evil for each person at birth. It was up to each person not to increase their apportioned evil by living a life of folly. The goddess Clotho spun the thread of life, Lachesis determined its length and assigned its destiny, and Atropos cut the thread of life at the end of one's days. In the face of such beliefs, Paul set forth the doctrine of the sovereignty and providence of a loving God. Trusting in God by faith is far better than clinging to life by a thread.

SALVATION'S GOLDEN CHAIN

Romans 8:29–30

In this lesson we delve into one of the deepest doctrines in the Bible.

OUTLINE

Christians can disagree energetically about the doctrine of election. Some say it turns humans into robots with no free will. Others say it's the only way to experience true freedom. What's the solution? As always, let the Scriptures speak for themselves.

I. **Salvation's Golden Chain**
   A. Link Number One: Foreknowledge
   B. Link Number Two: Predestination
   C. Link Number Three: Calling
   D. Link Number Four: Justification
   E. Link Number Five: Glorification

II. **Exploding the Myths About Election**
   A. Belief in the Doctrine of Election Promotes Arrogance
   B. Belief in the Doctrine of Election Promotes Anxiety
   C. Belief in the Doctrine of Election Promotes Apathy
   D. Belief in the Doctrine of Election Promotes Amorality

III. **Confirming the Truths About Election**
   A. Salvation's Golden Chain Was Created by God
   B. Salvation's Golden Chain Is Conceded by Everyone
   C. Salvation's Golden Chain Is Comprehended by No One

In this lesson we embark upon one of the most perilous journeys in the book of Romans. These two verses of Scripture contain, in a few words, a doctrine that has become the watershed between two different groups of Christians. Unfortunately, many pastors shy away from preaching this doctrine. But if we proclaim only those doctrines which are easy and which will cause no differences of opinion, we cannot be faithful expositors of the Word of God.

When he was preaching on 1 Thessalonians 1:4 ("knowing, beloved brethren, your election by God"), C. H. Spurgeon eloquently expressed my own heart on this issue:

> At the very announcement of the text, some will be ready to say, 'Why preach upon so profound a doctrine as election?' I answer, because it is in God's Word, and whatever is in God's Word is to be preached. 'But,' says the objector, 'some truths should be kept back from the people lest they make an ill use thereof.' That is popish doctrine! It was upon that very theory that priests kept back the Bible from the people. They did not give it to them lest they should misuse it. 'But,' says the objector, 'are not some doctrines dangerous?' Not if they are true and rightly handled. Truth is never dangerous. It is error and reticence, that are fraught with peril! 'But,' says the objector, 'Do not some men abuse the doctrines of grace?' I grant you that they do, but if we destroy everything that men abuse, we should have nothing left . . . . And, besides all this remember that men do read the Scriptures and think about these doctrines, and therefore make mistakes about them. Who then shall set them right if we who preach the Word hold our tongues about the matter?[1]

There are five great links in salvation's golden chain. The first two links are concerned with God's eternal counsel or past determination. The last two have to do with what God has done, is doing, or will do for us. The middle link, "calling," connects the first two with the last two.

SALVATION'S GOLDEN CHAIN
Link Number One: Foreknowledge

Often when I have heard people talk about the foreknowledge of God I have heard them say something like this: "Sure, God foreknows. He knows all, and since He knows all, then He knows who will believe and who will not, so it is accurate to say that God foreknows."

Another version of that interpretation goes like this: "Before the world was created God foresaw who were going to believe in Him and who would not. So on the basis of that foreseen faith, He decided to elect to salvation those good people who were going to exercise it."[2]

But such ideas are not possible if we really take the Bible at face value. The foreknowledge of God is much more than this for these reasons:

1. The object of God's foreknowledge is not the action of certain people but the people themselves. If all this word means is that God knows beforehand what people will do in response to Him or to the preaching of the gospel and then determines their destiny on that basis, what could God possibly have seen in any human heart but fixed opposition to Him (Romans 3:10–11)?

2. If God predestinates people because they are going to believe, then the ground of their salvation is in themselves and their merit and not in God and his mercy. John Murray said it this way: "Even if it were granted that 'foreknew' means the foresight of faith, the biblical doctrine of sovereign election is not thereby eliminated or disproved. For it is certainly true that God foresees faith; he foresees all that comes to pass. The question would then simply be: Whence proceeds this faith, which God foresees? And the only biblical answer is that the faith which God foresees is the faith that He Himself creates (cf. John 3:3–8; 6:44, 45, 65; Ephesians 2:8; Philippians 1:29; 2 Peter 1:2). Hence his eternal foresight of faith is preconditioned by his decree to generate this faith in those whom he foresees as believing."[3]

In other words, foreknowledge means that salvation has its origin in the mind or eternal counsels of God, not in man. It focuses our attention on the distinguishing love of God, according to which some persons are elected to be conformed to the character of Jesus Christ.

Link Number Two: Predestination

Foreknowledge and predestination are not the same. Predestination means to "pre-determine" someone's destiny. Think of predestination in terms of an airline flight to heaven:

Election is God deciding who gets on the plane bound for heaven. Predestination is his charting the route the plane will take, the schedule, the accommodations both during the flight and after the flight, and each passenger's safety. With God as the pilot of the plane and the plane itself, all who board the plane make it to heaven. Predesti-nation means God, himself makes sure the elect actually board the plane. Their response of faith in Christ is like checking in at the gate with a boarding pass.

The gospel call, in contrast, is like advertising for the trip. The church is commissioned to get the word to the whole world. Unfortunately most people treat God's free offer as 'junk mail' and throw it in the trash. However, those whom God has elected to salvation he also moves to accept his free offer. Many are called, but few are choen. Yet all who are chosen are predestined to end up in heaven.[4]

Foreknowledge is God fixing His love on the elect; predestination is His ensuring that the elect fulfill their destiny. John Stott makes this choice of God a very clear issue:

Clearly then, a decision is involved in the process of becoming a Christian, but it is God's decision before it can be ours. This is not to deny that we 'decided for Christ,' and freely, but to affirm that we did so only because he first 'decided for us.' Actually this choice was made in eternity past.[5]

He has determined that we will "be conformed to the image of His Son." In other words, God's goal for us is not just that we enter heaven at last, but that we be conformed to the image of God's Son. God's image was distorted by sin, but was restored in Christ, who was and is the image of God (2 Corinthians 3:18; 4:4; Ephesians 1:4; Colossians 1:15).

Paul says one of God's purposes in our predestination is that Christ might be the firstborn among many brethren. Barnhouse explains: "God the Father is so much in love with the Lord Jesus Christ that He determined that the whole universe should be peopled with sons made like unto this, the firstborn beloved Son. This is our glorification. This is the future of the one who believes in Christ."[6] Our being chosen for salvation includes being sanctified by the Spirit (2 Thessalonians 2:13; Hebrews 1:6; 2:11). We were predestined to be sanctified!

Link Number Three: Calling

There is both an outward and an inward aspect of our calling to be saved.

1. The Outward Call

   Some refer to this as the general or universal call that goes out to everyone to believe. No one of his own volition is able to answer this call (Matthew 11:28; John 6:44; 7:37).

2. The Inward Call

   This is also referred to as a specific or effectual call. With the call, the ability to respond is also given . God's inward call to salvation is effectively pictured in the resurrection of Lazarus (John 11). If a normal person stood before Lazarus' tomb and called him to come back from the dead, it would have been totally ineffectual. Lazarus would have remained dead. But when God Himself stands before the tomb and calls a person from death to life, it is an effectual, inward call. In the same way that Jesus called Lazarus from physical death to physical life, so God calls some from spiritual death to spiritual life.

Inward calling is the moment when that which was decreed in eternity becomes actual in time.

Link Number Four: Justification

Covered by Paul extensively in Romans, chapter 3, justification is simply the judicial act by which God declares sinful men and women to be in a right standing before Him, on the basis of what Jesus Christ did on the cross (Romans 3:24; 2 Corinthians 5:21).

Link Number Five: Glorification

Glorification means to be made like Christ. But note that Paul speaks of glorification in the past tense. We have been "glorified" already. Paul writes of this final step in our salvation as already having been accomplished. In the eyes of the One who has done this, we are already glorified! Griffith Thomas writes: "The tense in the last word is amazing. It is the most daring anticipation of faith that even the New Testament contains."[7]

EXPLODING THE MYTHS ABOUT ELECTION

Misunderstanding has led some to blame the doctrine of election for promoting carnal attitudes on the part of those who believe it. Rightly understood, the doctrine of election leads to just the opposite.

Belief in the Doctrine of Election Promotes Arrogance

It is sometimes argued that belief in election fosters pride--the elect bragging that they have been chosen by God while others haven't. In fact, the doctrine of election fills God's people with astonishment that He should have had mercy on undeserving sinners like themselves (Ephesians 1:5–6, 12, 14). Humbled before the cross, they desire to live the rest of their lives only to praise God.[8]

Belief in the Doctrine of Election Promotes Anxiety

The thought here is that people spend their whole lives in anxiety wondering whether or not they are the elect of God. But how can that be so? Most of the unbelievers I have ever talked with were not at all concerned with their status with God. Until the Spirit of God moves upon their hearts, they do not spend so much as one minute thinking about salvation at all. And believers who may, on occasion, experience doubt about their salvation have only to remember that their salvation rests in the power and keeping of God and their anxious thoughts are gone.

Belief in the Doctrine of Election Promotes Apathy

If salvation is all of God and not of man, the argument goes, then man has no responsibility at all and becomes passive in his concerns about spiritual things. Does the doctrine of election destroy freedom, and therefore responsibility, in man's experience? Sinclair Ferguson points out the clearest example we have of both election and freedom in the same man, the man Jesus Christ. No one's life was more predetermined than His, yet He was the most free man who ever walked on earth.[9]

One other aspect of the "apathy argument" says that if God is sovereign in salvation, we have no responsibility to evangelize the lost. Loraine Boettner's thoughts here are helpful:

> The decree of election is a secret decree. And since no revelation has been given to the preacher as to which ones among his hearers are elect and which are non-elect, it is not possible for him to present the Gospel to the elect only. It is his duty to look with hope on all those to whom he is preaching and to pray for them that they may each be among the elect In order to offer the message to the elect, he must offer it to all;

and the Scripture command is plain to the effect that it should be offered to all . . . .[10]

Belief in the Doctrine of Election Promotes Amorality

The argument here is this: If God has predestinated us to eternal salvation, then we cannot ever lose what God has guaranteed. So then, we can live as we want to, in sin and without restraint, for we will certainly be saved in the end. The problem with this view is that we have been predestined "to be conformed to the image of His Son" (Romans 8:29), "holy and without blame before Him" (Ephesians 1:4). A person chosen unto salvation will live a holy life.

CONFIRMING THE TRUTHS ABOUT ELECTION

Election becomes much more understandable when we summarize the essential truths about this important doctrine of the faith.

Salvation's Golden Chain Was Created by God

The longer we are Christians, the more we are aware of the fact that we had very little to do with our salvation. C. J. Vaughn underscores this truth:

> Everyone who is eventually saved can only ascribe his salvation, from the first step to the last, to God's favor and act. Human merit must be excluded: and this can only be by tracing back the work far beyond the obedience which evidences, or even the faith which appropriates, salvation; even to an act of spontaneous favor on the part of that God who foresees and foreordains from eternity all his works.[11]

Salvation's Golden Chain Is Conceded by Everyone

In his classic book, Evangelism and the Sovereignty Of God, J. I. Packer points out that, in reality, all Christian people believe in election and God's sovereignty in salvation, even if they deny that they do:

> Two facts show this. In the first place, you give God thanks for your conversion. Now why do you do that? Because you know in your heart that God was entirely responsible for it. You did

not save yourself; he saved you . . . . There is a second way in which you acknowledge that God is sovereign in salvation. You pray for the conversion of others . . . . You ask God to work in them everything necessary for their salvation. So our thanksgivings and our intercessions prove that we believe in divine sovereignty. On our feet we may have arguments about it, but on our knees we are all agreed.[12]

Salvation's Golden Chain Is Comprehended by No One

Many a person has ended up perplexed, if not frustrated, when trying to reconcile the truth of God's election of some yet His free over of salvation to all.

Now do not seek to mix these two things; and still more emphatically . . . do not try to 'reconcile' them! Profitless controversy and partisan feeling will be the only result. Who told us to 'reconcile' in our little minds, these seemingly contradictory things? Have we ceased to believe where we do not understand? . . . Now, if you undertake to 'reconcile' God's sovereign election with His free offer of salvation to all, you must sacrifice one truth or the other. Our poor minds may not 'reconcile' them both, but our faith knows them both, and holds both, to be true! And Scripture is addressed to faith, not to reason.[13]

In the final analysis, we rest in God's words as given to Isaiah: "For My thoughts are not your thoughts, nor are your ways My ways," says the Lord. "For as the heavens are higher than the earth, so are My ways higher than your ways, and My thoughts than your thoughts" (Isaiah 55:8–9).

Notes:

1. Cited by H. O. Van Gilder in an unpublished paper entitled "Election and . . . . ," 8.

2. William Hendriksen, *New Testament Commentary - Exposition of Paul's Epistle To The Romans* (Grand Rapids: Baker Books), 282.

3. John Murray, *The Epistle to the Romans* (Grand Rapids: Wm. B. Eerdmans, 1968), 316.

4. *Illustrations For Biblical Preaching*, Edited by Michael Green (Grand Rapids: Baker Book House, 1982), 117.

5. John R. Stott, *Men Made New: An Exposition of Romans 5–8* (Grand Rapids: Baker Book House, 1984), 101.

6. Donald Grey Barnhouse, *Romans, God's Heirs* - Romans 8:1–39 (Grand Rapids: Wm. B. Eerdmans Publishing Co, 1959), 175.

7. Griffith W. H. Thomas, *St. Paul's Epistle To The Romans* (Grand Rapids: Wm. B. Eerdmans Publishing Company, 1946), 226.

8. John Stott, *Romans: God's Good News For The World* (Downers Grove: Crossway Books, 1991), 250.

9. Sinclair B. Ferguson, "Predestination in Christian History," *Tenth: An Evangelical Quarterly* (October 1983), 7.

10. Loraine Boettner, *The Reformed Doctrine of Predestination* (Grand Rapids: Wm. B. Eerdmans Publishing Co., 1954), 285.

11. Cited by John Stott, 250.

12. J. I. Packer, *Evangelism And The Sovereignty Of God* (InterVarsity Press, 1961), 17.

13. William R. Newell, *Romans Verse By Verse* (Grand Rapids: Kregel Publishing Co., 1994), 331.

APPLICATION

1. Read Romans 3:10–18.

    a. Write down the evidence from these verses that God did not look down through history and choose those who had faith to be the elect:

       • Verse 10

       • Verse 11

       • Verse 12

       • Verse 13

       • Verse 14

- Verse 15

- Verse 16

- Verse 17

- Verse 18

b. Given the absence of faith in man, what is the only way that man could come to possess faith? (Ephesians 2:8–9)

2. Read John 6:44–45, 65.

   a. What is the only way a person can come to Jesus Christ?
      (verse 44)

   b. Who do you have to hear and learn from before finding
      yourself drawn to Christ? (verse 45)

   c. What would you say to someone who feels they have made a
      decision, in and of themselves, to accept Christ? (verse 65)

3. In addition to faith, what else has been granted to you by God?
   (Philippians 1:29)

   a. How does knowing this expand your concept of election?
      That is, in how many different ways have you been predestined
      to conform to the image of Christ? (Romans 8:29)

4. According to Ephesians 1:4, when were Christians chosen by God?

    a. For what purpose were they chosen?

    b. What was God's motivating "emotion" when He chose?

5. Read Colossians 1:15 and 2 Corinthians 3:18.

    a. If Christ is the firstborn, what does that imply others yet to be "born?"

    b. Who are those others? (Romans 8:29)

    c. Into whose image are we being transformed daily?

d. When you sin, how does it make you feel about the prospect of becoming conformed to the image of God in Christ?

e. What must you rely on in those moments instead of your feelings?

6. Read Mark 8:34; John 3:16, 7:37; and Revelation 22:17.

   a. What do each of these verses imply about the availability of salvation to all?

   b. What would you say to a person who wanted to be saved but was afraid God had not elected him to salvation?

DID YOU KNOW?

Election is the work of God, to be sure. But Scripture points out that man has a responsibility in election as well. Peter says, "Therefore, brethren, be even more diligent to make your call and election sure . . ." (2 Peter 1:10). Does he mean that it is up to us to make sure that we are among the elect? Not at all. Our election is a certainty by God's actions alone. Rather, Peter means the same thing as Paul meant when he said we are to walk in a manner worthy of our calling (Ephesians 4:1), and what James meant by saying that faith without works is dead (James 2:17). God does the electing, but we do the manifesting. He calls by His choice and we answer by our character (2 Peter 1:5–7).

FIVE UNSHAKABLE PROMISES

Romans 8:31–36

In this lesson we are reminded that nothing can separate us from the love of God.

OUTLINE

Some people worry about losing their salvation in the next life, while others worry about losing a sense of God's presence in the storms of this life. Both kinds of worry are unfounded. Nothing can cause the believer to fall outside the bounds of God's protective love in Christ.

I. **For the Believer in Jesus Christ There Is No Humiliation**

II. **For the Believer in Jesus Christ There Is No Deprivation**

III. **For the Believer in Jesus Christ There Is No Accusation**

IV. **For the Believer in Jesus Christ There Is No Condemnation**
   A. We Are Protected by Christ's Crucifixion
   B. We Are Protected by Christ's Resurrection
   C. We Are Protected by Christ's Exaltation
   D. We Are Protected by Christ's Intercession

V. **For the Believer in Jesus Christ There Is No Separation**

Some things are so wonderful that the only proper response is the response of silence. After presenting the wonderful truths of our relationship with God through the five links of salvation, Paul asks for a response—but he knows that there can be none. When he says, "What then shall we say to these things?" it is as if he is asking a question which cannot be answered. But in human terms, there are ramifications of the great truths of election and predestination he has just presented. And they are the focus of this lesson.

One commentator has said of verses 31–36, "This whole passage . . . strikes all thoughtful interpreters and readers as transcending almost everything in language."[1] Paul is undoubtedly talking about not only the things he has just presented in the preceding verses but all of the blessings that are ours in Christ. His question might be translated, "What is there left to say?"

John Stott sees Paul's interrogation like this:

The apostle's answer to his own question is to ask five more questions, to which there is no answer. He hurls them into space . . . in a spirit of bold defiance. He challenges anybody and everybody, in heaven, earth, or hell, to answer them and to deny the truth which they contain. But there is no answer. For no one and nothing can harm the people whom God has foreknown, predestined, called, justified, and glorified.[2]

In answering these five questions, we discover five unshakable promises that give us courage and hope in the midst of our fallen world. Rather than produce the outline in question form, I have chosen rather to emphasize the convictions that grow out of the questions. Just as there were five links in the chain of salvation (verses 29–30), so there are five convictions in these wonderful verses.

FOR THE BELIEVER IN JESUS CHRIST THERE IS NO HUMILIATION (8:31)

The way Paul asked this question, he is assuming a positive response. We could easily translate it this way: "Because God is for us, who can be against us?"

If Paul had simply asked, "Who can be against us?" there could be many answers to that question, some of which are listed in the last part of this passage. But the question is not "Who can be against us?" The question is "*If* God is for us, who can be against us?" What a big difference the little word *if* makes!

In other words, if anyone is able to take away our salvation, they would have to be greater than God Himself. In Romans 8:1 Paul tells us that for those who are in Christ Jesus, there is now no condemnation. Leon Morris expands on Paul's meaning:

> When Paul goes on to ask, 'Who can be against us?' he does not mean that the Christian has no opponents. His entire correspondence is eloquent of the foes the Christian encounters constantly. He means that with God 'for us' it makes not the slightest particle of difference who is against us. No foe can prevail against people who are supported by a God like that. The Christian's confidence is in God, not in anything he himself does, and for all eternity he can rely on God's gift. Paul is not speaking out of grim desperation, but in joyous elation.[3]

Paul's message is clear: If we were not able to do anything at all to save ourselves or to recommend ourselves to God in the first place, then what could we possibly do to ruin God's work in our lives. What we could not do, we cannot undo! But someone may ask, "Could God take away our salvation? Since He did it, could He undo it?" Paul's answer to that question is powerful: If God did not spare His own son in order to bring us eternal life, then would He allow His sacrifice to go for nothing? Would God do less for His children than He did for His enemies? Would He do less for us after we are saved than He did for us before we were saved?

FOR THE BELIEVER IN JESUS CHRIST THERE IS NO DEPRIVATION (8:32)

Since many Christians have read verse 32 many times, it is easy for us to take for granted the truth that it contains. Think for a moment about this thought:

> "God did not spare His own Son, but gave Him up for us all."

> God, the Judge, has a Son, an only Son, very precious to him. That Son never committed any sin. In all he did, He was ever pleasing to His Father (John 8:29) . . . Yet, on this precious and beloved Son, God now pronounces the sentence we deserved. It is a sentence immeasurable in its severity, and is carried out in every detail . . . . He, the Son, fully bore that horrendous curse. He drank the cup of unspeakable agony to the very last drop. That bitter cup, Love drank it up. It's empty now for me.[4]

Paul's argument is this: If God's love for us compelled Him to give up His own Son in our behalf, is there anything that He will fail to do to keep us? Horatius Bonar captured this thought in these poetic lines:

What will He not bestow?
Who freely gave this mighty gift unbought,
Unmerited, unheeded and unsought,
What will He not bestow?

He spared not His Son!
'Tis this that silences each rising fear,
'Tis this that bids the hard thought disappear.
He spared not his Son![5]

William R. Newell suggests that we use this truth in our prayers. He says that we should come to God like this: "Thou didst not spare Thy Son, but gavest Him for me. Now I need a thing from Thee; and I ask it as one to whom Thou gavest Christ!"[6]

The word "freely" is the Greek word *charizomai*. It comes from the root word meaning "grace." It means to bestow grace freely and abundantly. That is how God gives to His own. This word is often used to describe the manner in which believers are to forgive one another (Ephesians 4:32). It is probable that this is what Paul had in mind here as well.

FOR THE BELIEVER IN JESUS CHRIST THERE IS NO ACCUSATION (8:33)

In the last book of the Bible, Satan is called the "the accuser of our brethren" (Revelation 12:10). But even though the world and Satan are always bringing charges against God's people, those charges cannot stick because the One who justifies is also the One who is the judge. Marcus Rainsford does away with every possibility of condemnation when he writes:

There is no ground for condemnation since Christ has suffered the penalty; there is no law to condemn us since we are not under law but under grace; there is no tribunal for judgment since ours is now a Throne of Grace, not a judgment; and above all, there is no Judge to sentence us since God Himself, the only Judge, is our justifier."[7]

I recently was read this story which illustrates the power of Paul's words:

A little boy was shooting rocks with his slingshot. He could never hit his target. As he returned to Grandma's backyard, he spied her pet duck. On impulse he took aim and let fly. The stone hit, and the duck was dead. The boy panicked and hid the bird in the woodpile, only to look up and see his sister watching.

After lunch that day, Grandma told Sally to help with the dishes. Sally responded, 'Johnny told me he wanted to help in the kitchen today. Didn't you Johnny?' And she whispered to him, 'Remember the duck!' So Johnny did the dishes.

What choice did he have? For the next several weeks he was at the sink often. Sometimes for his duty, sometimes for his sin. 'Remember the duck,' Sally'd whisper when he objected.

So weary of the chore, he decided that any punishment would be better than washing more dishes, so he confessed to killing the duck. 'I know, Johnny,' his grandma said, giving him a hug. 'I was standing at the window and saw the whole thing. Because I love you, I forgave you. I wondered how long you would let Sally make a slave out of you.'[8]

Johnny had been listening to the words of his accuser and had become enslaved by his words. More than a few of God's children have had the same experience. Paul reminds us that for us who have been freed by the death of Christ, there can never again be a valid accusation.

FOR THE BELIEVER IN JESUS CHRIST THERE IS NO CONDEMNATION (8:34)

Now comes another question: "Who is he who condemns?" And the answer is 'No one.' As believers, we have a four-fold protection in Christ.

We Are Protected by Christ's Crucifixion

Christ died on the cross and took for us the condemnation that we deserved. We cannot be condemned because He has already been condemned for us! He is the propitiation for our sins (Romans 8:3; Galatians 3:13; 1 John 2:2).

We Are Protected by Christ's Resurrection

When He came back from the grave, Christ proved His victory over sin and over death. And it is not just the fact that He rose from the dead, but that He was raised from the dead by the Father. This demonstrates that the Father was satisfied with the sacrifice of His Son as the only basis for our justification. His resurrection is the proof of our justification (Romans 4:24–25).

We Are Protected by Christ's Exaltation

He is even now at the right hand of God. The exaltation of Jesus Christ to the right hand of God the Father symbolizes the honor, power, and authority given to Him as a reward for His fully accomplished work (Psalm 110:1; Philippians 2:8–9). In the Old Testament temple there were never any seats because the work of the priests in dealing with sin was never done. But here we are told that when Christ was exalted, He sat down! The work is done! There will never again need to be a sacrifice for sin (Hebrews 1:3; 10:11–12).

We Are Protected by Christ's Intercession

The power of Christ's endless life saves us to the uttermost (Hebrews 7:25; 1 John 1:9; 2:1)! Hodge writes: "His very presence at the Father's right hand is evidence of his competed work of atonement, and his intercession means that he continues to secure for his people the benefits of his death."[9]

FOR THE BELIEVER IN JESUS CHRIST THERE IS NO SEPARATION (8:35–36)

When Paul speaks of the love of Christ, he is not talking about our love for Christ but of His love for us. He points to Christ's love for us as a safeguard against the difficulties of life. Our love for Him is fickle, His love for us is steadfast (1 John 4:9–10, 19):

What kinds of circumstances does Paul have in mind as he speaks of being separated from Christ? He lists seven threats which might come against the believer, though there could obviously be more. None of them can separate us from God.

1. Tribulation. This is the Greek word *thlipsis*. This word and its verb form are used 37 times in the New Testament to describe the direct troubles that afflict the believer. The word means to be squeezed or put under pressure. It describes the pressures that are brought against one from the outside.

2. Distress. This translates the Greek word *stenochoria*. This is a compound word, made up of two words which mean narrow and space. It conveys the idea of being hopelessly hemmed in, to be in strict confinement. First Corinthians 10:13 tells us that God will make a way for us to escape such temptations and will give us the strength to stand up under the stress.

3. Persecution. This is the Greek word *diogmos* and it is used ten times in the New Testament and always in reference to the gospel. The verb means to make to run or to run swiftly to catch those who are pursued. So the word is translated persecution. Jesus talks about this circumstance in the Beatitudes (Matthew 5:10–12).

4. Famine. The word famine, Greek *limos*, is found 12 times in the New Testament. Only twice is it associated with believers (here and in 1 Corinthians 11:27). Famine is usually the result of persecution. According to the book of Revelation, this will be a common cause and effect relationship in the last days.

5. Nakedness. This is not a reference to complete nudity but to the poverty that keeps a person from adequately clothing himself. Paul experienced this as a result of living in stressful circumstances while spreading the gospel (1 Corinthians 4:11).

6. Peril. In 2 Corinthians 11:26 Paul used this word eight times to describe the various kinds of peril he had experienced: Peril from waters, robbers, his countrymen, Gentiles, in the city, in the wilderness, in the sea, and among false believers. The word peril means to be constantly in harm's way. It is a reference to danger, treachery, and mistreatment in general.

7. Sword. This is a special kind of sword. It is not the long sword that was used in battle, but rather the short assassin's sword. This circumstance is more likely to be murder than execution. A casual reading of 2 Corinthians 11 will demonstrate that Paul was not talking in theory only: ". . . he had already suffered the first six of these seven hardships before writing this epistle to the Romans. . . . By means of the seventh . . . the sword, he was going to be put to death. The apostle was speaking not only by inspiration but also from experience, therefore, when he stated that none of these things can bring about separation between believers and their Lord, he knew what he was saying."[10]

In closing this section the great apostle quotes from Psalm 44:22.

Paul cites [these words] to bring out the truth that for God's people there is real risk and a call for real devotion. Christians might be tempted to think that became the love of Christ is so real and so unshakable they need not fear that they will run into trouble. Scripture shows that, while the love is sure, so are troubles. For the sake of God we face death all day long. Actually Paul says something stronger than this: 'We are being killed all day long.' It is real and not imaginary peril that Christians face.[11]

And yet, with the nearness of God's protection, we are safe. Brenning Manning tells the story of an Irish priest who, on a walking tour of a rural parish, sees an old peasant kneeling by the side of the road, praying. Impressed, the priest says to the man, "You must be very close to God." The peasant looks up from his prayers, thinks a moment, and then smiles, "Yes, he's very fond of me." [12] The sovereign grace of God is surely something in which the believer rests and rejoices. God is for us!

Notes:

1. Quoted by William R. Newell, *Romans Verse By Verse* (Grand Rapids: Kregel Publishing Co., 1964), 334.

2. John Stott, *Men Made New-An Exposition of Romans 5–8* (Grand Rapids: Baker Books, 1984), 254.

3. Leon Morris, *The Epistle To The Romans* (Grand Rapids: W. B. Eerdmans, 1988), 335.

4. William Hendriksen, *New Testament Commentary - Exposition of St. Paul's Epistle To The Romans* (Grand Rapids: Baker Books, 1980–1).

5. Quoted by Kent Hughes, *Romans - Righteousness From Heaven* (Wheaton: Crossway Books, 1991), 170.

6. William R. Newell, 337.

7. Quoted by Griffith Thomas, *St. Paul's Epistle To The Romans* (Grand Rapids: Baker Books, 1946), 230.

8. Cited by Max Lucado, *In The Grip Of Grace* (Dallas: Word Publishing Co., 1996), 176.

9. Charles Hodge, *A Commentary On Romans* (Edinburgh & Carlisle: The Banner of Truth Trust, 1972), 290.

10. William Hendriksen.

11. Leon Morris, 339.

12. Phillip Yancey, *What's So Amazing About Grace?* (Grand Rapids: Zondervan, 1997).69.

APPLICATION

1. How do the three descriptions of God in Psalm 27:1 serve as a source of protection for the believer?

   a. Light:

   b. Salvation:

   c. Strength:

2. Read Psalm 46:1–3.

   a. What do the descriptions in verses 2–3 represent? That is, are they literal or figurative?

   b. What is a refuge? (verse 1)

   c. What refuge did God provide for Noah and his family at the time of the Flood? (Genesis 6:14 ff.)

   d. How is the Lord like a refuge, an ark, in times of trouble?

e. Describe a time in your spiritual life when you found yourself running to the Lord as a refuge from the trouble around you:

3. Read Isaiah 40:22–28.

a. What is the overall theme of the passage? How is God being described?

b. What is His relation to the heavens and the earth? (verses 22, 26)

c. What is His relation to the princes and inhabitants of the earth? (verses 22–24)

d. Who, or what, in earth is found to be His equal? (verse 25)

e. How likely is it that God could ever be caught "off guard" by a challenger? (verse 28)

f. What are the implications of this passage for the protection of the believer?

4. When God gave us His Son, what was accomplished? (Galatians 3:13)

   a. Could the demands of the Law have ultimately separated us from God had Christ not come?

   b. Can the demands of the Law separate us from God since Christ has taken the punishment of the law for us?

   c. How does 1 John 2:2 say that Christ has solved the sin problem for believers?

   d. How much of the world could potentially find protection from the world's troubles in Christ?

   e. If God took it upon himself to remove the primary thing separating us from Him—the curse of the Law—how much more can we trust that He is able to protect us from lesser things?

5. Read Hebrews 11:35–38.

   a. List the different ways saints in the Old Testament suffered in their walks with God:

b. Did they, in this life, receive the fulfillment of all the promises God had made to Abraham? (verse 39)

c. What did God have in store for them instead? (verse 40)

d. How does suffering in this life fit in with our protection in God's love?

e. What can those united to God through Christ expect to experience in this life? (2 Timothy 3:12)

DID YOU KNOW?

In Romans 8:36 Paul compares Christians to sheep. But not just any sheep—sheep being led to slaughter. It is well known that sheep are not the most discerning of creatures. They will follow a lead sheep or a shepherd blindly into danger—even the slaughterhouse. Sometimes it may appear that God's people are being led into suffering and He is nowhere around to defend or protect them. But that is never the case! If one, or many, of God's people suffer harm on this earth, it is with His permission, not because of His inattention. God's love binds His people to Him eternally. So the next time you think you have walked blindly into a slaughterhouse, remember: Your Shepherd is leading you all the way and is there to see you through.

CONQUERING SHEEP

Romans 8:37–39

In this lesson we discover all the things we are protected from when in Christ.

OUTLINE

Deep down, everyone is tempted to be afraid of something. The past, the future, powerful people, supernatural forces, death—there is a lot to consider. But the Christian considers only one thing: Nothing—nothing—is more powerful than the love of God in Christ Jesus.

I. **The Victorious Pronouncement**

II. **The Victorious Persuasion**
   A. Not the Crisis of Death nor the Calamities of Life
   B. Not the Intervention of Angels nor the Intrusion of Demons
   C. Not the Cares of Today nor the Concerns of Tomorrow
   D. Not Afflictions From the Heavens nor Advances from Hell
   E. Powers
   F. Any Other Created Thing

III. **The Victorious Conclusion**
   A. Our Enemies Are Not Human but Spiritual
   B. Our Struggle Is Not Momentary but Constant
   C. Our Victories Are Not Earthly but Eternal
   D. Our Rewards Are Not Perishable but Permanent

J ohn Chrysostom, the early church father, was given his name
because of his eloquence. His name actually means, "The
Golden-mouthed." He was born in A.D. 345 to wealthy parents.
His mother was widowed at the age of 28 and refused to remarry
so that she could devote all of her time to the education of her son.
His education was the finest available in his day. After his mother
died in 374, John Chrysostom practiced a severely ascetic life for
the next six years. He actually lived in a cave on a mountain near
Antioch. Chrysostom lived a pure and simple life that was a rebuke
to his wealthy parishioners. He was a giant in moral and spiritual
stature and ended life in such a fearless way that even the Roman
Emperor was no match for him.

When Chrysostom was brought before the Roman Emperor,
the Emperor threatened him with banishment if he remained a
Christian. Chrysostom replied, 'Thou canst not banish me, for
this world is my father's house.' 'But I will slay thee,' said the
Emperor. 'Nay, but thou canst not,' said the noble champion
of the faith, 'for my life is hid with Christ in God.' 'I will take
away thy treasures.' 'Nay, but thou canst not for my treasure
is in heaven and my heart is there.' 'But I will drive thee away
from man and thou shalt have no friend left.' 'Nay, thou canst
not, for I have a friend in heaven from whom thou canst not
separate me. I defy thee: For there is nothing that thou canst do
to hurt me.'[1]

John Chrysostom was a champion in his day. Paul says that we,
too, are champions. In fact we are more than champions—we are
more than conquerors!

THE VICTORIOUS PRONOUNCEMENT (8:37)

What does Paul mean when he refers to believers as more than
conquerors? The phrase "more than conquerors" is actually the
translation of one Greek word. That word is *hypernikomen*. The
middle part of the word, nikao, means to overcome. Nike was the
name given to the goddess of victory in Ancient Greece. The word
hyper means "over and above." So when you put the two words
together you get the meaning—"over and above victory." Believers
are super-conquerors. And note that this is present tense, not future
tense. We are at present more than conquerors.

And we are:

not merely conquerors, so that the forces that oppose us are neutralized . . . but more than conquerors, so that death, life, angels, principalities, things present, things to come, heights and depths, yes every created thing that has anything to do with us, works in our favor, for in all of them, and in the manner in which they affect us, there is revealed to us the love of God which is in Christ, a love from which no one and nothing will ever be able to separate us.[2]

Martyn Lloyd-Jones gives this added description of what it means to be more than conquerors: We are not simply enabled by His love to hold on, and not to fall away and falter; neither is it the case that we just manage to obtain a victory. We are 'more than conquerors,' a very strong expression! The Christian is not a man who manages somehow or another just to obtain an entrance into heaven. He is 'more than conqueror.' He not merely stands up to these trials, he demolishes them, he is enabled to overcome them completely. He not merely conquers them, he is 'more than conqueror'. And let us not forget that death is included. Everything that can possibly come against us is included.[3]

James Montgomery Boice makes an interesting observation about this verse in his commentary on Romans: We have just been reminded in the previous verse, by a quotation from the Old Testament, that the people of God, 'face death all day long' and are considered as sheep to be slaughtered' (Psalm 44:22). But now in verse 37, we are told that nevertheless we are all 'more than conquerors.'

Sheep that conquer? We can think of lions that conquer, or wolves or polar bears or wild buffalo. But the very idea of sheep as conquerors seems ludicrous. This is figurative language, of course. But the image is not meaningless, nor is it as ludicrous as it seems. In contrast to the world and its power, Christians are indeed weak and despised. They are helpless as a flock of sheep. But they are in fact conquerors, because they have been loved by the Lord Jesus Christ and have been made conquerors 'through him.'[4]

When Paul talks about these things he is referring to all the things that have been listed in the previous section plus all the things that he is about to enumerate. He makes it very clear indeed that this conquest is due to God's love for us. When we place Romans 8:28 alongside Romans 8:37 and note the similarities, we will see this divine love:

8:28 "And we know that all things work together for good to those who love God . . . ."

8:37 "Yet in all these things we are more than conquerors through Him who loved us."

Verse 28 says that this promise is for those who love God. But verse 37 reminds us that we can only love Him because He first loved us. The love of God and the love of Christ are one. God's love for his own is the center piece of this whole chapter. This is why Paul says that we are more than conquerors.

THE VICTORIOUS PERSUASION (8:38)

Paul begins this section with "we know" (verse 28) and he ends the section with the more personal "I am persuaded" (verse 38). This latter phrase is in the perfect tense in the Greek language and could be translated, "I have become and I remain convinced." There is a big difference between knowing a truth and being persuaded of it.

To know a Bible truth, you have only to read it: to be 'persuaded of it in the Lord Jesus' involves the fact, first, that the truth in question touches your own personal safety before God; and, second, that your heart has so been enlightened by the Holy Spirit, and your will so won over—'persuaded'—that confidence, heart-satisfied persuasion results.[5]

Paul's persuasion is not only the result of his knowledge of God's truth but it is also the product of his own experience. He has experienced most of the things that he is writing about and now that he has come through them, he can say with confidence that none of them can separate him from God's love.

He is not saying all this simply because he happens to have a particular feeling in him at the moment. Neither is he just hoping—hoping against hope. What he says is, 'I am certain.' It is interesting to note that he puts this in the passive, 'I am persuaded,' which means 'I have come, through a process of persuasion, to a settled conclusion.' That is the true content of the phrase. He does not persuade himself; something else has persuaded him. He is passive. The result is that, as the result of this process of persuasion, he has come to a settled conclusion; he is certain. It is an absolute certainty, beyond any doubt whatsoever.[6]

To make his point, he selects ten items (four pairs and two singles) which could possibly become a barrier between us and Christ.

Not the Crisis of Death nor the Calamities of Life

Paul was not frightened of death. He knew that Christ had eliminated death's power for those who were in Christ: "The last enemy that will be destroyed is death . . . . 'O Death, where is your sting? O Hades, where is your victory?' The sting of death is sin, and the strength of sin is the law. But thanks be to God, who gives us the victory through our Lord Jesus Christ" (1 Corinthians 15:26, 55–57). Not only was death incapable of separating the apostle from Christ, but life also stood powerless to do so. Some feel that life poses a much greater threat in this regard than death. For many, life is much more difficult than death. Burdens, bitterness, disappointments, uncertainties, physical miseries; all of these things could pull one away from Christ is He were not in control (1 Corinthians 15:31; 2 Corinthians 5:8; Philippians 1:21, 23; 2 Timothy 1:10; Hebrews 2:14–15; Revelation 1:17–18).

Not the Intervention of Angels nor the Intrusion of Demons

Many writers believe that the mention of angels in verse 38 is a reference to evil angels. They argue that no good angel would ever attempt in any way to separate a believer from His Lord, an interpretation I agree with. Whether good or bad, however, it matters not because Paul says angels are powerless to do anything to remove us from the love of God.

The reason for this is obvious. Christ reigns over all the angels of heaven, all principalities and powers, and all are powerless to harm those who He loves (Ephesians 1:20–22; Colossians 2:14; 1 Peter 3:21–22).

Not the Cares of Today nor the Concerns of Tomorrow

Paul says that on the continuum between the present and the future, there is nothing that can separate us from the love of God. From verses such as Romans 8:31 ("If God is for us, who can be against us?"), and 8:33 ("Who shall bring a charge against God's elect?") we have already discovered that things in the present cannot harm us (see also 8:34; John 16:33; 1 John 5:4).

And nothing in the future can sneak up on us either because the Bible says that Jesus Christ is in complete authority over the future: "'All authority has been given to Me in heaven and on earth'" (Matthew 28:18).

Not Afflictions From the Heavens nor Advances From Hell

Paul's reference to heights and depths calls to mind David's words in Psalm 139:8: "If I ascend into heaven, You are there; If I make my bed in hell, behold, You are there." In other words, God is at the top and the bottom of the universe and everywhere in between. There is nothing in that "vertical" realm which can harm us.

Powers

This word is the word *dunamis* in the Greek language. In the plural form, this word often refers to miracles or mighty deeds. It was also used figuratively of persons in positions of authority and power. Whatever Paul meant by this word, it is just another way of describing an obstacle that could be a serious problem if we were not super-conquerors.

Any Other Created Thing

Since only God Himself is uncreated, everyone else and everything else is excluded. This is a comprehensive statement that makes sure that nothing is left out of Paul's list. Everything is under the control of God the Creator and the Lord Jesus Christ and so nothing will be able to separate us from the love of God that is in Christ Jesus our Lord.

John Stott summarizes the assurance Paul's words bring: "Nothing seems stable in our world any longer. Insecurity is written across all human experience. Christian people are not guaranteed immunity to temptation, tribulation or tragedy, but we are promised victory over them. God's pledge is not that suffering will never afflict us, but that it will never separate us from his love."[7]

THE VICTORIOUS CONCLUSION

To bring our study to a conclusion, let me offer four reasons why Christians are more than conquerors through Jesus Christ.

Our Enemies Are Not Human but Spiritual

"For we do not wrestle against flesh and blood, but against principalities, against powers, against the rulers of the darkness of this age, against spiritual hosts of wickedness in the heavenly places." (Ephesians 6:12)

If our enemies were human as we are our victories would not be anything special. Because our enemy is who he is, when we are victorious, it is a super victory. Satan is not the opposite of God, he is the creature of God. But he is a very powerful creature and his strategies against God's sheep are formidable. If it were up to us we would never be able to stand against the enemy of our souls. But through Jesus Christ we are more than conquerors.

Our Struggle Is Not Momentary but Constant

Donald Grey Barnhouse makes this point:

In earthly battles, soldiers are sometimes called upon to fight day and night. But there comes a moment when flesh and blood cannot take more and the struggle comes to an end through the utter exhaustion of the soldier. But in the spiritual warfare there is no armistice, no truce, no interval. The text is in the present tense . . . in the Greek. 'For thy sake we are being killed all the day long.' From the moment we are made partakers of the divine nature, we are the targets of the world, the flesh and the devil. There is never a moment's reprieve. It follows, then, that our conquest is more than a conquest, and thus we are more than conquerors.[8]

And the victory is this: In this constant struggle, we are made better not worse. We come out of our troubles stronger than when we went into them (Romans 5:3–5; 2 Corinthians 12:9).

Our Victories Are Not Earthly but Eternal

Every victory that we win in the natural or human realm will one day seem unimportant to us. Most human victories are buried in the graves of the victors. But the battles that we are fighting have eternal ramifications: "For our light affliction, which is but for a moment, is working for us a far more exceeding and eternal weight of glory, while we do not look at the things which are seen, but at the things which are not seen. For the things which are seen are temporary, but the things which are not seen are eternal" (2 Corinthians 4:17–18).

Our Rewards Are Not Perishable but Permanent

No matter what happens to us in the race we run on earth—we may grow weary, we may be injured, we may fall down—nothing will keep us from receiving the prize of an imperishable crown which lasts forever: "Do you not know that those who run in a race all run, but one receives the prize? Run in such a way that you may obtain it. And everyone who competes for the prize is temperate in all things. Now they do it to obtain a perishable crown, but we for an imperishable crown" (1 Corinthians 9:24–25).

Romans, chapter 8—39 verses of pure promise for all who have placed their faith in Jesus Christ. I trust before you leave this great chapter you will make sure you are among those predestined to be conformed to the image of Christ and to live under His protection. Being "in Christ Jesus" (Romans 8:1) is simply a matter of faith in Him.

Notes:

1. Quoted by Kent Hughes, *Romans - Righteousness From Heaven* (Wheaton: Crossway Books, 1991), 171.

2. William Hendriksen, *New Testament Commentary - Exposition of St. Paul's Epistle To The Romans* (Grand Rapids: Baker Books, 1980), 301.

3. D. Martyn Lloyd-Jones, *Romans - Final Perseverance of the Saints - Exposition of Chapter 8:17–39* (Grand Rapids: Zondervan Publishing Co., 1975), 444.

4. James Montgomery, *Romans - Volume Two - The Reign Of Grace* - Romans 5–8 (Grand Rapids: Baker Books, 1992), 991.

5. William R. Newell, *Romans Verse By Verse* (Grand Rapids: Kregel Publishing Co., 1964), 345.

6. D. Martyn Lloyd-Jones, 448.

7. John Stott, *Romans - God's Good News For The World* (Downers Grove: InterVarsity Press, 1994), 259.

8. Donald Grey Barnhouse, *God's Heirs: Exposition of Bible Doctrines, Taking The Epistle of Romans As A Point of Departure,* Vol. 7, Romans 8:1–39 (Grand Rapids: Wm. B. Eerdmans, 1963), 202–203.

1. What do we have (present tense) in the world according to Jesus' words in John 16:33?

    a. Why is it possible to be of good cheer in spite of that reality?

    b. What does it mean that Jesus has "overcome the world?"

    c. What does it mean to you personally? That is, what situation are you facing in your life which is part of living in this world, which Jesus says He has overcome? Fill in the sentence below from John 16:33 with the situation you are facing:

    d. "Be of good cheer, I have overcome _____."

2. Why should you give thanks to God according to 1 Corinthians 15:57?

    a. What has God given us the victory over? (1 Corinthians 15:55)

    b. What does Paul say in Romans 8:38 that is consistent with this victory?

    c. Is death something you will gain victory over when you die, or is death something you have victory over now?

    d. How should the life of a person be different knowing that death is (present tense) a defeated foe?

3. In 2 Corinthians 2:14–16, what does Paul give thank to God for? (verse 14)

    a. As we walk in triumph (victory) in Christ, what is released through us? (verses 14–15)

    b. What impact does our walk in victory have on those around us? (verses 15–16)

    c. If we are a Christian, yet are not walking in the protection and victory secured for us by Christ, how might the impact of our life be reversed on believers and unbelievers?

4. Read Romans 5:3–5.

    a. In this life, why are we able to glory in the tribulations we endure?

    b. Is the end result of our position in Christ that our tribulations are removed?

    c. What is the last thing we develop in tribulations? (verse 4)

    d. Which is better—to have tribulations removed or to have hope?

    e. Why is hope better? That is, on what is hope based? (verse 5)

5. What must one do in times of difficulty to experience the power of Christ resting upon him? (2 Corinthians 12:9)

   a. How does living in weakness correspond with living under the protection of God's love in Christ? (Romans 8:39)

   b. What area of your life is an area of weakness for you?

   c. What must you do to experience the reality of Christ's power to sustain you?

   d. What will happen if you try to be strong in the flesh at the same time Christ wants to be strong in you? (Galatians 5:17)

DID YOU KNOW?

Roman armies would march triumphantly into Rome when returning from victorious military campaigns. The generals would lead a procession of soldiers and captives through Rome to the cheers of the citizens. The air would be filled with the sweet smell of incense and spices which were burned as part of the celebration. Paul uses that image to picture the victory march being led by God of all those who have placed their faith in Christ. Because we have been made victors over everything in Christ, our lives should release a sweet fragrance which is the knowledge of Christ to all who witness our procession. Are you part of the parade or are you observing the parade? God has won the victory. All it takes to be part of the procession is faith in Jesus Christ the Lord.

Romans Volume 1:
God's Righteousness & Man's Rebellion
Chapters 1 – 3

In this study of Romans chapters 1 – 3, Dr. Jeremiah makes sure you understand life's most important question—"How can a man be righteous before God?" (Job 9:2)—and more importantly, the answer.

Romans Volume 2:
Man's Ruin & Christ's Redemption
Chapters 4 – 7

This second volume in Dr. Jeremiah's *Living by Faith* series traces Paul's logical and theological discussion of sin, servitude, and victory over the flesh. It is a study in doctrine and theology that will change your life forever.

Romans Volume 3:
The Sons of God & the Spirit of God
Chapter 8

So deep and rich is Romans 8 that this entire volume is devoted to plumbing its depths. Join Dr. Jeremiah as he takes you verse by verse through one of the greatest presentations of the spiritual life in all of Scripture.

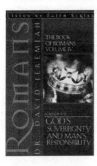

Romans Volume 4:
God's Sovereignty & Man's Responsibility
Chapters 9 – 11

Follow along with Dr. Jeremiah through some of the most challenging texts in all of Scripture. Studying Romans 9 – 11 will give you new reasons to stand amazed at the wisdom and purposes of God.

Romans Volume 5:
Loving God & Living Godly
Chapters 12 – 14

What does a living sacrifice to God look like? In this volume, Dr. Jeremiah's clear and practical exposition of Romans 12 – 14 will encourage you to become a living sacrifice to God. You'll discover that the mercy of God is more than just theology; it is the motivation for a life of total commitment to Christ.

Romans Volume 6:
Staying Together & Reaching Out
Chapters 15 – 16

Dr. Jeremiah concludes an exhaustive study of Christendom's most important letter with this last volume. These final chapters of Romans include Paul's admonitions on unity in the church and reveal his passion for people.

with Dr. David Jeremiah

Each series is also available with correlating CD audio albums.

For pricing information and ordering, contact us at www.DavidJeremiah.org or call (800) 947-1993.

STAY CONNECTED
TO DR. DAVID JEREMIAH

Take advantage of two great ways to let Dr. David Jeremiah give you spiritual direction every day! Both are absolutely FREE.

Turning Points Magazine and Devotional

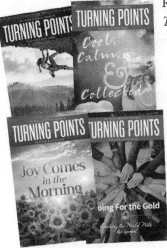

Receive Dr. David Jeremiah's magazine, *Turning Points,* each month:

- Monthly study focus
- 48 pages of life-changing reading
- Relevant articles
- Special features
- Daily devotional readings
- Bible study resource offers
- Live event schedule
- Radio & television information

Daily Turning Point E-Devotional

Start your day off right! Find words of inspiration and spiritual motivation waiting for you on your computer every morning! Receive a daily e-devotion communication from David Jeremiah that will strengthen your walk with God and encourage you to live the authentic Christian life.

There are two easy ways to sign up for these free resources from Turning Point. Visit us online at www.DavidJeremiah.org and select "Subscribe to Daily Devotional by Email" or visit the home page and find Daily Devotional to subscribe to your monthly copy of *Turning Points.*